Milan Goved

Me, As A Penguin

by Tom Wells

Co-commissioned by
Milan Govedarica and West Yorkshire Playhouse

**First showcased at West Yorkshire Playhouse
on 28 April 2009**

**First performance at Arcola Theatre, Studio 2, London,
on 27 April 2010**

Tour dates
Arcola Theatre, London, April 27–May 22
The Octagon, Hull, May 24
The Lowry, Studio, Salford Quays, May 27–29
West Yorkshire Playhouse, Courtyard Theatre, Leeds, June 10–12

Me, As A Penguin

Cast
in order of appearance

STITCH	**Ian Bonar**
LIZ	**Samantha Power**
MARK	**John Catterall**
DAVE	**Daniel Abelson**

Production Team

Writer	**Tom Wells**
Director	**Chris Hill**
Designer	**Barney George**
Lighting Designer	**Dan Hill**
Sound Designer	**Andrew Thomson**
Stage Manager	**Calum Clark**
Lighting Technician	**Leo Woolcock**
Press & Publicity	**Jane Verity**
Publicity Designer	**Laura Jukes**
Production Photography	**Alexandru Boicu**
Casting Consultant	**Kay Magson CDG**
University of Leeds Placement	**Katherine Hughes**
Producer	**Milan Govedarica**

Foreword

I first encountered Tom Wells in 2007. At West Yorkshire Playhouse I run an annual new-writing course somewhat provocatively titled So You Want To Be A Writer? To apply, aspirant playwrights have to write a letter about themselves, why they want to write and why they want to join the course. Over seven years and well over 600 applications there are only a handful I can still remember and even fewer that I can still quote from verbatim. Tom's is one of those. In cramped but careful handwriting (his computer was broken apparently) he told a plaintive and achingly funny tale of penning sad poems by the banks of the Humber estuary. Over the five weeks of the course he was a shy and retiring presence, whose modest manner belied the bold, touching and occasionally ribald pieces he produced.

The idea of So You Want To Be A Writer? is to identify as yet untried and unknown writers with the talent and determination to write for theatre. Tom was selected, along with a number of others from this group, first to write a ten minute two-hander for site specific performance and then to take part in a series of masterclasses led by Associate Artist Colin Teevan. The challenge to the participants was to write a full-length play, which, if we liked it, would have a rehearsed reading. The play Tom delivered was Me, As A Penguin, more or less the play you see here. It was, he said, a play inspired by a knitting magazine and a newspaper story about a school trip to a zoo. It was helped along its way by a supportive but analytical session with Roxana Silbert, then Artistic Director of Paines Plough, and a rehearsed reading directed by Kathryn Ind, ITV Trainee Director.

Together with It's A Lovely Day Tomorrow by two other SYWTBAW graduates, Dom Grace and Boff Whalley, Me, As A Penguin was selected to be part of Northern Exposure 2009. This has been West Yorkshire Playhouse's season of new writing and new work from across the North. This double bill of two new plays generated by our new writing schemes sat alongside new work by Imitating the Dog, New Writing North and Unlimited Theatre. The idea of Northern Exposure is to showcase work rather than fully produce and I had two weeks to direct both plays with four very hard-working actors performing both. That it worked as well as it did is a testament to the strength of the writing and the talents of the actors: John Catterall and Samantha Power who here return to the roles of Mark and Liz, Tom Hudson as Stitch and Robin Simpson as Dave.

Nearly exactly a year to the day after the first show in Leeds, Me, As A Penguin opens in its first full production at the Arcola, London before a tour taking in Hull, Salford and back to West Yorkshire. From a one page letter, through workshops, readings and finally the world (okay, a UK tour); it is immensely satisfying to see the progression of a writer and play through inception to creation. This, I'm sure, is only the beginning of Tom's journey as a writer and hopefully it will also be an inspiration to other aspiring writers. Who knows? Maybe this play will be seen by someone who also wanders lonely along the estuary dreaming of being a writer and another journey will begin.

Alex Chisholm
Associate Director (Literary)
West Yorkshire Playhouse

Cast and Crew

Daniel Abelson (DAVE)
Theatre credits include: *Country Magic* (Finborough Theatre); *A Midsummer Night's Dream* (Opera North); *Goodbye My Love* and *The One That Hurts The Most* (Southwark Playhouse); *Macbeth* (West Yorkshire Playhouse); *Saving Sam* (Royal Court International Residency); *Shadow of a Gunman* (Glasgow Citizens Theatre); *The Cow Play* (Oxford Playhouse Studio); *5/11*, *King Lear*, *The Government Inspector*, *A Midsummer Night's Dream*, *Seven Doors*, *Thermidor*, *Unopened Doors*, *Holes In The Skin*, *The Man With The Flower In His Mouth* and *The Seagull* (Chichester Festival Theatre); *Sunken Eyed Boy* (Manchester Contact Theatre), *Wise Guys* (Red Ladder) and *Romeo and Juliet* (Creation Theatre). TV credits include: *Doctors* and *Nice Guy Eddie* (BBC); *The Royal Today* (ITV) and *Robin Hood* (Tiger Aspect/BBC). Radio credits include: *On The Field*, *The Draw*, *The Paston Letters*, *Out of the Pirate's Playhouse* and *Thea's Diary* (BBC).

Ian Bonar (STITCH)
Trained at Bristol Old Vic Theatre School 2001-04. His theatre credits include: *Beauty and the Beast* (Told by an Idiot); *The Miracle* and *DNA* (National Theatre); *Ma Vie En Rose* (Young Vic); *Flat Stanley* (West Yorkshire Playhouse); *Beyond Omarska* (White Bear); *Aladdin* (Bristol Old Vic) and *Anorak of Fire* (Diorama Studio). Ian's TV credits include: *Going Postal* (Sky); *Holby City* and *New Tricks* (BBC); *Teenage Kicks* (Philip McIntyre Productions); *The Green, Green Grass* (Shazam); *Hotel Babylon* (Carnival Films); *Totally Frank* (Endemol UK/ Channel 4) and *What You Looking At* (Raw TV/Channel 4). His film credits include: *Tintin* (Paramount Pictures); *1-2-3-4* (Carson Films); *How To Lose Friends and Alienate People* (Alienate Films); *Inkheart* (New Line Cinema); *Atonement* (Tallis Pictures); *Starter for Ten* (Scamp/Playtone/HBO).

John Catterall (MARK)
Since graduating from UCLan in 2006, John has done a variety of work across different media. His theatre credits include: *Beep* (Theatre in the Mill); *Me, As A Penguin* and *It's a Lovely Day Tomorrow* (West Yorkshire Playhouse/Northern Exposure); *Company Along the Mile* (Milan Govedarica/West Yorkshire Playhouse) and *Tom Sawyer* (The Dukes Lancaster). Film and TV credits include: *Emmerdale*, *Coronation Street* and *Heartbeat* (ITV); *Doctors*, *All The Small Things*, *Beautiful People* and *Holby City* (BBC); GI Jonny (BBC Online); *Vincent*, *Forsyte Saga*, *Girls In Love* and *Children's Ward* (Granada); *Peak Practice* (Carlton), *Playing The Field* (Tiger Aspect) and *Boy A* (Cuba Pictures/Channel 4). John recently made his radio debut for BBC Radio 4 in *The Granny Killers*, and has subsequently recorded several other productions for the BBC and independent producers.

Calum Clark (Stage Manager)
Calum returns to the team having previously worked on *Born In Bethlehem* by Al-Harah Theatre and *Company Along the Mile* by Tom Bidwell. A self-proclaimed Jack Of All Trades (master of none), he co-founded Liverpool

stilt-walking street-theatre troupe, Artemis, in 2001. He is also an actor, sound designer and multi-instrumentalist and was last seen lighting and treading the boards with Chumbawamba on the Riot, Rebellion and Bloody Insurrection tour 2009/10. He has been company stage manager with Red Ladder Theatre Company since 2007.

Barney George (Designer)

Barney works regularly as a designer for the stage as well as for short films. Design credits for the stage include *The Worm Collector*, *Cinderella*, *Full of Noises* and *Mela* for West Yorkshire Playhouse; *Beep* for Northern Bullits; *They Only Come at Night* and *Resurrection* for Slunglow; *Company Along the Mile* (Milan Govedarica in association with WY Playhouse); *Squawk Box* for Hook & Eye and *Precious Bane* for Interplay Theatre. Design for film includes an award-nominated version of *Romeo and Juliet* made in collaboration with Rosie Coles, a visual artist with a learning disability, and *This Way Up*, directed by Sarah Punshon. He is also a regular contributor to Leeds-based community projects. His individual approach can also be seen in solo performance pieces and live events made in collaboration with other artists. He was a founding member of the performance collective, Rabbit, with Tassos Stevens.

Chris Hill (Director)

Chris trained on the MFA in Theatre directing at Birkbeck and at the Guildhall School of Music and Drama. He was Director on attachment to ArtsEd's Acting department in 2007 and to the West Yorkshire Playhouse in 2008/2009. Directing credits include: *Osterley* (Urban Scrawl Radio Project) *DUST* and *Kidnapping Agatha* (West Yorkshire Playhouse); *Roald Dahl's The Witches*, *One Flew Over the Cuckoo's Nest*, *Sweeney Todd* and *West Side Story* (Edinburgh Festival) as well as a number of readings at West Yorkshire Playhouse and Arch 468 as part of their script development programmes. Assisting includes: *Swanhunter* (Opera North and tour) *Il Signor Bruschino* and *La Scala di Seta* (BYO), *Bedroom Farce*, *Othello*, *Peter Pan* and *Don't You Leave Me Here* (West Yorkshire Playhouse).

Dan Hill (Lighting Designer)

Dan has nationwide experience in lighting design for theatre, live music, dance and corporate events. Theatre lighting design credits include: *Riff Raff* (Arcola Theatre); *A Day at the Racists* (Finborough Theatre); *Spam and Beans the Wedding* (Roundhouse Studio); *Woyzeck* (Embassy Theatre); *Jake's Women* (White Bear Theatre); *Holiday Romance* (Etcetera Theatre); *A Dublin Carol* (Bridewell Theatre); *Closer* (Barbican Theatre, Plymouth); *Die Fledermaus* (The Drum, Plymouth); *Love of the Nightingale* (Embassy Studio) and *Oklahoma* (Putney Arts Theatre). Theatre assisting credits include: *The Rake's Progress* and *Il Signor Bruschino & La Scala di Seta* (Peacock Theatre); *Mrs Warren's Profession* (Bath Theatre Royal); *Full Monty* (English Theatre Frankfurt) and *Sweet Charity* (Menier Chocolate Factory). Dan was recently announced the winner of the Michael Northen Bursary Award 2009 for his lighting design for *Woyzeck* (Embassy Theatre). He is graduating from the Central School of Speech and Drama in summer 2010.

Samantha Power (LIZ)

Theatre credits include: *Loving Peter Palmer* (Lost One Act Festival/Ripley), *Flintstreet Nativity* (Everyman Theatre), *Little Britain Live* (UK and Australian tour); *It's a Lovely Day Tomorrow*, *Coming Around Again* and *Accrington Pals* (West Yorkshire Playhouse); *Street Trilogy, Kid* and *Raw* (Theatre Absolute); *Little Malcolm* (Bolton Octagon); *Educating Rita* (Brighton); *School Daze* (Riverside Studios); *The Importance of Being Earnest* and *Spring and Port Wine* (national tours) and *Iron* (Working Girls/Contact, Manchester). Television credits include: *Moving On, Lunch Monkeys, Heatbeat, The 370, Shameless, Massive, The Cup, Little Britain, Doctors, It's Adam and Shelly, New Street Law, Twisted Tales, The Royal, Barbara, Where the Heart Is, The Cops, The Safe House, City Central, Peak Practice, A Prince Among Men, No Bananas, Coronation Street* and *Spoofovision*. Film credits include: *Mischief Night* and *The Low Down*. Radio credits include: *Little Britain* (series 1&2).

Andrew Thomson (Sound Designer)

After his theatre debut in late 2009 on *Beep* by Aisha Khan & Mark Catley at Theatre in the Mill, *Me, As A Penguin* is Andrew's first touring production. As a sound designer, Andrew has worked in film, television, radio and theatre, he is also a music producer working with BAFTA award-winning clients. 2010 sees him hoping to pass on his production knowledge via a series of masterclasses hosted by Future Arts in Leeds.

Jane Verity (Press & Publicity)

Jane has been working at West Yorkshire Playhouse for two and a half years. This is her first freelance project. She also writes short fiction, and was shortlisted for the Cadaverine Award at last year's Ilkley Literature Festival. In September she will start an MA in Creative Writing at Manchester University.

Tom Wells (Playwright)

Tom grew up in Kilnsea, East Yorkshire. *Me, As A Penguin* is his first full-length play. He took part in West Yorkshire Playhouse's So You Want to Be a Writer? programme in 2007 and was selected for Paines Plough's Future Perfect attachment in 2009. Other writing credits include *About a Goth* for Oràn Mór in Glasgow and *Notes for First Time Astronauts* for Later at Soho Theatre.

Milan Govedarica
Producer

Milan is a theatre producer based in West Yorkshire specialising in creating and touring productions by new and international artists. His interest is in bringing together young artists to create fresh, original plays with wide, diverse appeal. His last production, *Company Along the Mile* by Tom Bidwell, directed by Justin Audibert, played to packed houses in Leeds, London and Manchester in 2009. In the last five years he has collaborated with some of Yorkshire's best new artists, including Aisha Khan, Jodie Marshall, Mark Catley and Alan Lane.

Another part of his work is introducing international artists to UK theatres and audiences. In 2007 he was one of the people who brought the award-winning Belarus Free Theatre to the UK for the first time. He has an ongoing association with BFT, producing performances in a secret location in Leeds in 2008 in association with West Yorkshire Playhouse and holding international workshops with them in UK and Athens in 2009. In 2008 he produced a UK tour by Palestinian theatre company Al-Harah with their production *Born In Bethlehem*, a rare opportunity to see Palestinian theatre in the UK. He has also brought over artists from Serbia, Greece, Hungary and Romania to lead workshops in this country.

Originally from Belgrade, Serbia, Milan spent six years working for the National Theatre of Belgrade where he helped to set up and run NADA (NovA DramA) Project, the only project in Serbia for new writing. There he helped organise workshops, readings and international exchanges. Many of the playwrights NADA backed, worked with and advocated for finally had their plays produced in Serbia and abroad.

Milan lives in Leeds with his wife and daughter.

www.milangovedarica.com

Production thanks to:

Mark Hollander at ACE Yorkshire; Red Ladder Theatre
Company; Dick George Associates; Lisa Evans at
Guildhall School of Music and Drama;
John and Kitty Chisholm; Elisa Amesbury;
Patrick Howson; Marion Nuttall; Jonny Walton.

The Author would like to thank:

Mel Kenyon and Rachel Taylor; Chris Hill and Milan
Govedarica; Daniel Abelson, Ian Bonar, John Catterall,
Sam Power and everyone working on the production;
Alex Chisholm, Dom Grace, Boff Whalley and Kathryn
Ind; Tessa Walker and Owen Whitelaw; Jane Fallowfield
and Ben Webb; Lu Cardey, Laura Lomas, Danielle Sibley,
Adam Taylor and Penny Skinner; Sarah Cunningham and
Tom Walmsley; Claire Battershill, Katy Knight, Adèle Allen
and Charlie Boss; Cheryl and Nan.

Lastly, love and special thanks to Mum, Dad and Ruth.
For your patience, your kindness and your cupboard.

Yorkshire activities of *Me, As A Penguin* tour are supported by
the National Lottery through Arts Council England

LOTTERY FUNDED

ME, AS A PENGUIN

Tom Wells

Characters

STITCH, *timid, in a cardigan*
LIZ, *not timid, pregnant*
MARK, *well-meaning but worried*
DAVE, *unimpressed, dressed as a giant penguin*
SAM, *offstage*

This text went to press before the end of rehearsals and so may differ slightly from the play as performed.

ACT ONE

Casting On

'Beginning anything new can be daunting, and knitting is no exception. Mistakes made while casting on can trouble you right through to a garment's completion. Take care, and take your time. Imagine the finished piece. Nothing spurs a young girl on to success more readily than the thought of a well-knitted bedsock.'

A Girl's Guide to Knitting & Crochet, Janice Thripp (1962)

Scene One

*A room with a sofa. A door at the back leads to the bathroom,
from which splashing is heard. STITCH comes out of the
bathroom, damp, with a worried expression. He shuts the door,
leans against it, looks up and sighs.*

STITCH. Bugger.

> STITCH *sits down on the sofa and starts knitting. His
> expression is approaching shell shock. A Transformers
> lunchbox rests on the floor by his feet, and next to the sofa is
> a rolled-up sleeping bag and a bag stuffed haphazardly with
> clothes. In front of the sofa is a low table with a CD player
> and some chunky headphones. On the back wall is a
> telephone. LIZ enters, heavily pregnant, waddles over to the
> sofa and sits down (heavily).*

LIZ. I want this bump out. Now.

STITCH. I'm sorry.

LIZ. It's so uncomfortable. And I need the loo.

STITCH. No help with that either I'm afraid.

LIZ (*starts to get up*). Oh, well. If you want something doing…

STITCH (*holds onto her*). No, Liz. You can't.

LIZ. I've had three mango lassis, Stitch. I can't not.

STITCH. It's just.

LIZ. Like drinking sunlight at the time. Now this.

STITCH. Sam's in there. Had a bit of an accident earlier. He's
having a bath.

LIZ. Poor lad. He had one at the jumble sale and all. They sent
him home in floral culottes.

STITCH *smiles*.

It's not funny.

STITCH. No, just. It wasn't that sort of accident.

LIZ. Oh. Oh God, is he alright?

STITCH. Yeah, he's fine. Just a bit. Wet.

LIZ. What happened?

STITCH. Well, you know. Not much. Fell in with the penguins. A bit.

LIZ. What was he doing in with the penguins?

STITCH. That's what I thought.

LIZ. You were looking after him.

Pause. STITCH *shrugs*.

Remind me never to let you take the bump out.

STITCH (*smiling*). Thought you wanted it out. Now.

LIZ. I meant to, wherever you've been. Feed it to the sodding lions, you will. Then shrug.

STITCH. No lions.

LIZ. Whatever, tigers.

STITCH. Liz, it's an aquarium. The penguins are only there for half-term.

LIZ. They must have something in the way of predators.

STITCH. Squids, I suppose. They're quite shifty-looking.

LIZ. What do they eat?

STITCH. Dunno. Fish maybe. Seaweed. When I was there this bloke tried feeding the stingrays Battenberg. They weren't keen.

Beat.

LIZ. I could just eat a bit of Battenberg.

STITCH. Well. You're in luck.

LIZ. Wahey.

STITCH. Mum sent one with me for the journey. Should be just in my bag down there. Can you reach?

LIZ looks in STITCH*'s bag at the side of the sofa. She takes out a few crumpled T-shirts, then finds a bottle of pills, looks at them quickly and puts them back. She finds the Battenberg.*

LIZ. Got it. Oh, hang on. You don't think it'll make matters worse.

STITCH. Nah, probably soak a bit up. Looks quite absorbent really. For a snack. I'll get a knife.

LIZ (*who has already bitten into the whole thing*). You're alright. I'll manage like this.

Pause. LIZ *chews thoughtfully.* STITCH *examines his knitting.*

I love Battenberg.

STITCH (*carries on knitting*). Mm.

LIZ. D'you think you could live off it?

STITCH. You seem to.

LIZ. I meant for ever though.

STITCH. Don't see why not. Sponge. Jam. Marzipan. Three of your five-a-day.

LIZ. Odd though, isn't it? Wonder who first thought: cake's okay, but. Taste better in a grid. And it does. Sort of genius, that.

Pause. STITCH *is still knitting.*

Okay. If the biggest risk is a squid, you can take the bump out when it's ready.

STITCH. Cheers.

LIZ. Not the penguins though.

STITCH. I didn't push him in.

LIZ. Well, why was he there in the first place?

STITCH. It's complicated.

LIZ. If it takes my mind off my bladder, I'm in.

STITCH. Fine. Dave was there. Working.

LIZ. Who?

STITCH. You know. Mark's mate. I met him Saturday.

LIZ. Oh, that Dave.

STITCH. He let us in to help feed them.

LIZ. I didn't realise he worked there.

STITCH. Yeah. Travels round with the penguins. Various places.

LIZ. Come on then, what happened?

STITCH. Well, I didn't know it was him, to begin with.

LIZ. Must've looked different without the vodka.

STITCH. I suppose. He was dressed as a giant penguin though, so.

LIZ. Really?

STITCH. Some sort of promotional thing.

LIZ. Dressed up as a giant penguin.

STITCH. Enormous, yeah.

LIZ. And you still fancy him?

STITCH (*quietly*). Mm.

    Silence.

LIZ. Give it time, eh. Eh?

STITCH. I am.

    Silence.

    Seemed quite pleased to see me.

LIZ. Great.

STITCH. Mm.

LIZ. Sounds nice.

STITCH. I suppose he is, yeah. Knows his sea life.

Quite sweet, really, the other night. He told me about these penguins in New York. Gay penguins. When all the others, the straight ones, were looking after the eggs and that, they looked after this stone. He said they kept it warm, kept it safe. Every year they did their best to hatch it. Didn't work though. Then one year, the zookeepers swapped it, the stone, for an egg. It'd been, you know. Sorted. And they hatched it. Dads. Like the others. Just, family.

(*Embarrassed.*) It's a nice story, anyway. Don't know if it's… Think he might've been.

LIZ. What? Making it up.

STITCH. No. (*Bashful.*) Chatting me up.

LIZ *reacts*.

I know.

LIZ. So, today was like a date?

STITCH *shakes his head*.

STITCH. Just a coincidence.

LIZ. Really?

STITCH. No, not really. That's why I took Sam. In case I looked like a stalker.

LIZ. And did you?

STITCH. I hope not. Think I played it quite cool really.

LIZ (*looking doubtful*). Great.

STITCH. Yeah.

Pause.

I did do something stupid. I mean. Sort of. You'll laugh, anyway.

LIZ (*uncertain*). Yeah?

STITCH. Oh, it doesn't matter. Tell you later.

Pause.

LIZ. Look, Stitch. I don't want to tell you what to do or anything. I'm not some sort of bossy big sister. You know best
and that. And to Dave's credit, I've never met him so I might
be wrong but. The thing is. I won't lie. Most of Mark's
friends are. I dunno how to describe them really. Complete
twats?

STITCH. Oh.

LIZ. Dave might be different. He's gay, I suppose, which sort of
bucks the trend a bit. No idea Mark was so open-minded.
What next – vegans? Still. I just want to say now, at the start:
you go steady. Alright? Be careful. And don't get too…

STITCH. I won't, I won't. I just. You know.

LIZ. Good to hear. (*Pause.*)

How long does it take to have a sodding bath? (*Shouting.*)
You alright in there, Sam? He's alright in there, isn't he? On
his own?

STITCH. I'm sure he's fine.

LIZ. Very quiet.

STITCH. Just tired I think. Long day and that. Eventful.

LIZ. You don't think he's fallen asleep?

STITCH. He'll just be getting warm. The penguin water was
fairly chilly.

LIZ. I am going to have to go soon. Bump's cranking up the
pressure. It's sort of bouncing at the moment.

STITCH. Can I feel?

LIZ. Course.

STITCH *puts his hand on the bump.*

STITCH. Oh. (*Beat*.) Oh.

It's so sweet.

LIZ *snorts*.

Oh, right. Sorry. Probably not that comfy for you, sacred vessel. Maybe it's the curry kicking in, though. Did you get something hot?

LIZ. Vindaloo.

STITCH. Brilliant. That'll have it out like a shot.

LIZ. Stitch, I want a baby, not a missile.

STITCH. I know but. Still. Good effort.

LIZ. Not really. Mark had most of it. I just had a peshwari naan and a Rennie. I'm not fussed about spicy food to be honest. And the indigestion I've had lately. Mark thinks I'm fussing. Moody git.

STITCH. Where is Mark?

LIZ. Don't ask. There's nowhere to park outside so he dropped me off at the door and now he's circling the one-way system like a vulture. Never seen anyone look so menacing in a Renault Clio. Still. Do him good to have some time on his own.

STITCH. Have you two fallen out? (*Pause*.) What's the matter?

LIZ. Oh, nothing, just. Keep your head down for a bit.

He'll want the loo and all. (*Shouting, as MARK enters*.) Sam, your Uncle Mark'll be in in a bit, he's in a shocking mood, you might want to start getting dry.

MARK *stands still, unimpressed*. LIZ *adds, as an afterthought:*

He's had a curry.

Fade.

Scene Two

LIZ *is still sitting on the sofa, next to* STITCH, *who is now knitting.* MARK *is standing by the bathroom door, scowling. He sighs a number of times. After the third sigh,* LIZ *sighs.*

MARK. This is bloody ridiculous.

> (*Hammering on door*.) Hurry up in there, Sam, alright.

LIZ. Leave the poor lad alone. (*Shouting*.) You take your time in there, Sam.

MARK. Was there any need for that?

LIZ. I don't want him to slip or anything.

> *Pause.* STITCH *continues to knit.*

MARK. How long's he been in there? (*Pause*.) Stitch?

STITCH (*stops knitting*). Pardon?

MARK. How long's he been in there?

STITCH. Oh, um. Not too long. I'm not sure, though. A while, I suppose. He'll be out. Some time.

> STITCH *starts knitting again.*

MARK. Thanks. Helpful.

LIZ. Don't have a go at Stitch just cos you need the loo. We wouldn't be having this trouble if you'd let us save up for an en suite like I said –

MARK. Oh, don't go on about –

LIZ. Well, it's true, you wouldn't have any of it, and now –

MARK. I've heard this enough times –

LIZ. All you'd talk about was that bloody Nintendo Wii.

> *Beat.*

MARK (*quietly*). Leave the Wii out of it, Liz.

LIZ. I'm just saying.

MARK. Well, it's not helpful, is it? You wouldn't've got an en suite anyway, you told me that.

LIZ. I might've.

MARK. You said you wanted a new settee.

LIZ. Could've had both.

MARK. How d'you figure that one out?

LIZ. When you were working at IKEA we could've got a big discount on a sofa. A nice Scandinavian sofa. And Sam's dad would've done the plumbing on the en suite for free, he said that.

MARK. Only cos he fancies you.

LIZ (*sighs*). Well, we're getting a new settee when the baby comes. This one's no good for a baby, it'll stain. And it's ugly. We need beige.

MARK. Beige. Right. (*Smiling.*) I'll remember that. If you ever get round to having the sodding thing.

LIZ (*smiling*). Don't push it.

MARK. One of us has to.

LIZ (*laughs, then suddenly serious*). Don't make me laugh.

MARK. This is silly. (*Knocks on door.*) Sam, is it alright if I just nip in for a wee? Cheers.

STITCH (*jumping up, vaulting sofa to stop* MARK). No!

MARK. What?

STITCH. You better not.

MARK. Why?

STITCH. He just. Gets shy. I'll go, um. Get him dry and that.

STITCH *slips into the bathroom, closes the door in* MARK*'s face and locks it.*

MARK. What just?

MARK tries the door.

 Locked.

He kicks it, but not too hard, and comes to the sofa. Sits down heavily, on STITCH*'s knitting, and jumps up again.*

Oh, bloody. Ow. This has to stop.

LIZ. Just look where you're sitting.

MARK. How come he can go in there and I can't?

LIZ. Stitch'll help. You'd. I dunno.

MARK. I'd what?

LIZ. Boys get embarrassed seeing grown men's bits. Even yours.

MARK. He could look away.

LIZ. He's seven, he wouldn't look away. Point and laugh maybe, but. (MARK *smiles*.) Just: be patient. It's all good practice anyway. Good Dad practice.

Pause. MARK *picks up the knitting again. It is a fairly indistinct shape.*

MARK. Wonder what this is.

LIZ. Yeah.

MARK. D'you not know?

LIZ. Scarf, maybe.

MARK holds it at arm's length, unsure.

Maybe something for the bump.

MARK. D'you think the bump'll be into knitting?

LIZ. Maybe.

MARK sighs.

What?

MARK. Nothing. It's just. It's a bit odd, isn't it?

LIZ. It's a good skill. Knit all sorts. Stitch is always wearing. Stuff.

MARK. So are we.

LIZ. I mean, good stuff he made himself. That cardi: I think it's really original.

MARK. Definitely.

LIZ. I mean it. There's a bit of himself in the stuff he makes. Not just the time and that but, you know, his little worries. Little decisions. The stuff we wear's probably made by some poor orphan in a sweatshop somewhere. Probably swapped that T-shirt for grains of rice. Vaccinations. Like wearing guilt, that is. I don't want the bump dressed up in guilt.

MARK. So you want Stitch to teach it to knit?

LIZ. Course I do.

MARK. Really?

LIZ. Yes.

MARK. Even if it's a boy?

LIZ. Oh. Not if it's a boy. Bloody hell.

MARK. Why not?

LIZ. Just be a bit. Kooky.

Pause.

MARK. What is he doing in there? How long does it take to dry a child?

LIZ. You know Sam, he's. Thorough. And Stitch isn't a mile a minute.

MARK. He shot in there.

LIZ. Yeah.

MARK. Bit odd really.

LIZ *is quiet.* MARK *takes a deep breath.*

I really think it's time he went home.

LIZ. Let him put some clothes on first.

MARK. I meant Stitch.

LIZ *sighs*.

What?

LIZ. We've been through this once tonight. He's not going anywhere.

MARK. That's the trouble.

LIZ. Stitch isn't trouble. I'm not kicking my brother out when you won't even get rid of the settee.

MARK. The settee's special. If my brother turned up I'd soon send him packing. In his pinstripe suits with his bloody, I dunno. Career.

LIZ. Enough.

MARK. Anyway, we can't throw the settee out while someone's sleeping on it.

LIZ. So. (*Smiling.*) While the settee stays, Stitch stays. And while Stitch stays, the settee stays. This is shaping up nicely.

MARK. You're an infuriating woman.

LIZ. Cheers.

The phone rings. Neither MARK nor LIZ move. They just sit, facing forward on the sofa. Wait three rings, then:

LIZ. You'll have to answer it, love, I can't move.

MARK. It'll be your mum.

LIZ. I can't get up.

MARK. Course you can.

LIZ. Mark, honestly. I'm not sitting down, I'm beached.

MARK. I can soon give you a heave up.

LIZ. If you're getting up can you not just answer it? Please?

MARK (*sighs*). Alright.

He starts to get up as the phone clicks onto answerphone.

No point now, really.

LIZ (*excited*). Shh.

ANSWERPHONE. Hello?

SAM (*on the phone*). Hi, Aunty Liz.

ANSWERPHONE. Just kidding. Liz and Mark are out, leave us a message. Beep.

LIZ (*laughing*). Every time.

MARK. Hang on.

SAM (*on the phone*). Mum, it's the answermachine. (*Mum says something in the background.*) Hi, um. Hello. I forgot my lunchbox. It's red with Transformers on. What? (*Mum says something.*) I meant pardon. (*Mum says something else.*) Mum says she'll pop round and pick it up tomorrow. And you're not to worry about it. Love from Sam.

Click. Long silence.

LIZ. Bloody hell.

MARK. Who's in the bathroom then?

Fade.

Scene Three

LIZ *stands at the bathroom door and listens for a moment.*

LIZ. He's definitely talking to someone.

MARK. You're kidding?

MARK *also listens.*

He's just humming.

LIZ. Stitch. Are you coming out then?

STITCH. Just a minute.

LIZ. We've had Sam on the phone. Says he forgot his lunchbox.

Pause.

STITCH. Oh. Right.

LIZ. Will you come out then, talk to me?

STITCH. No, I don't think I will.

MARK. Let me try.

LIZ. Just. Be patient.

Why won't you come out here? Mark's bursting.

STITCH. I just, um. I don't want to.

LIZ. But why, though?

Silence.

Stitch, whatever it is. Just say it.

STITCH *mumbles something.*

MARK. Well, say it so we can hear it.

LIZ. Mark.

Silence.

STITCH. I don't want to go back to the shop. You'll send me home.

LIZ. We won't send you home, Stitch.

STITCH. You will in a bit.

LIZ. We won't. Will we, Mark?

Silence. MARK *nods 'yes'.*

Mark says no. He says stay as long as you like. Just open the door, Stitch. We're. We're a bit worried about you.

Silence. Eventually, the door unlocks. STITCH *slides out, not meeting anybody's eye.* MARK, *muttering, goes into the bathroom and locks the door.* STITCH *sits down, picks up his knitting and starts, concentrating hard.* LIZ *sits down next to him.*

You're forever knitting. Do you not miss the shop?

STITCH *shrugs.*

Mum says they're missing you. She says everyone who comes in asks after you. Lily and Ivy and, that woman off the caravan site. With a limp. Shaves her eyebrows off then draws them back in felt tip.

STITCH. Dot.

LIZ. They keep bringing in stuff they can't finish. Mum says they didn't realise how good you were till you'd gone. They'll have to pay you more when you go back. Is that why you came? Were they taking your knitting for granted?

STITCH. No.

LIZ. Well, what then?

STITCH *doesn't say anything. Neither does* LIZ.

STITCH. It's silly really.

LIZ. Tell us then. While Mark's not here to put his foot in it.

Pause.

STITCH. It was just sort of spur of the moment. I'd spent all afternoon trying to realign Mrs Stothard's pinking shears cos her grandson set about them with a WWE wrestling figure. Triple H, I think. She bought some pink lambswool with a thread of silver running through it and a pattern to crochet an ornamental loo-roll cover. Like a ball gown. You stitch half a Barbie on the top.

LIZ. Classy.

STITCH. Mm. I thought to myself, I'm twenty-two, I shouldn't be doing this. We had the radio on, just in the background. And I caught the words to this song. Bit different to my usual stuff but. Anyway. It was the most beautiful song, all about like yearning and not belonging and that. It was perfect, like it was written just for me that minute. Sort of spoke to me across time. Quite: deep.

LIZ. What was it called?

STITCH. 'Funky Town'. By Lipps Inc.

LIZ. Eh, it's a good one, that. Mark's got it on a party mix somewhere, hang on.

LIZ jumps up and starts looking through a stack of CDs.

STITCH. Anyway, that night after we closed, I packed my stuff, got on the bus and sort of. Came here.

LIZ. To Funky Town.

STITCH. Well, Hull but. It'll do. I just. I just want a go, at it. The whole gay thing. Just, dip my toe in, test the water sort of. I can't do that at home. There's nothing. No bar or. Not even a book club. Two lesbians who keep tropical fish and a paedophile ring, they think that's enough for a seaside town but. It's not for everyone, is it? It's not for me.

LIZ. Is Hull any better?

STITCH (*lacking a bit of conviction*). I'm already doing better. Loads better. With Dave. I mean, I think I am.

LIZ. Mm.

LIZ puts the CD into the CD player.

Are you dancing with me then?

STITCH. You're alright.

LIZ. What's up with you? Love a dance, you.

STITCH. Not tonight.

LIZ. Come on, it'll be like in *Pulp Fiction*.

STITCH (*doubtful*). Just like it, yeah. I thought you needed the loo.

LIZ. It'll help me forget. Anyway, might get the bump moving. Come on, Stitch, do your bit for the bump.

STITCH. No.

LIZ. Why not?

STITCH. Dunno.

LIZ. I remember when we couldn't stop you dancing. That's
how we twigged, you know. A few blue Smarties, you were
off like Billy Elliot.

STITCH *doesn't move*.

Oh love, what's the matter?

STITCH. Nothing. I'm just, a bit down.

LIZ. We all get a bit down, Stitch. That's why there's dance
routines. Come on, shoes off, we'll do it properly. You'll
have to be Uma, though, I'm far too pregnant.

STITCH *gets up, still not keen*.

STITCH (*sadly*). I'm always sodding Uma.

LIZ. Properly, I said. For me.

*They take their shoes off and face each other. LIZ switches
the CD on and they dance. STITCH does as he is told, and
manages a sultry, suitably Uma-ish performance. LIZ is a bit
too pregnant and a bit too enthusiastic for John Travolta, but
she tries. They look like they've done it before. After a little
while, MARK appears. He stands for a moment, watching
from the bathroom doorway. LIZ is oblivious, but STITCH
freezes. He looks worried. MARK turns the music off,
stopping LIZ in the middle of an attitude-filled front crawl.*

What're you doing? We're dancing the bump out.

MARK (*quietly*). I think you should come and see this, Liz.

LIZ. Mark. Whatever you've done just. Keep flushing.

MARK. It's not that, it's. I've found something. Behind the
shower curtain. Just, just come.

*LIZ and MARK go into the bathroom. STITCH sits down
and starts knitting, anxiously.*

LIZ (*from bathroom*). Bloody hell! Stitch? Stitch?

Fade.

ACT TWO

Dropping Stitches

'Even the most experienced knitters make mistakes: you can only do your best. When all's said and done, a dropped stitch isn't the end of the world, though it might mean a hole in your gym knickers.'

A Girl's Guide to Knitting & Crochet, Janice Thripp (1962)

Scene One

STITCH *sits on the sofa, knitting.* LIZ *stands up, cross.* MARK
sits on the arm of the sofa, patting her, as if to calm her down.

LIZ. This is what you'd call playing it cool?

MARK. At least you can go to the loo now.

LIZ. With that watching? Hardly. It could pounce. What were
you thinking?

STITCH *shrugs.*

You'll have to do better than that.

STITCH. I don't know, do I? It just sort of. Happened.

(*Making a fist around the knitting and gesturing.*) What do
you want me to say?

MARK. Nothing, Stitch, it's fine, just. Put the knitting down.

STITCH. Sorry. (*He does.*)

I can't remember much. Dave let me and Sam in to help feed
them. He loved it, Sam. They were all taking the fish out of
his hand and that, real friendly. Quite loud too. But then
there was this young one that wasn't getting any fish. It was
smaller than the others, a bit scruffy-looking. A bit: dim.
Like just being there was taking quite a lot of effort. And, I
don't know. I just. It was like looking in a mirror. There I
was. Me. On the edge a bit. Not getting any. Fish.

Then Sam fell in. Everyone was watching that. I sort of
thought: now's my chance. Scooped it into his *Transformers*
lunchbox and came straight home. Didn't put up a fight or
anything. Don't think it's got a lot of fight.

MARK (*amused*). Fair play.

LIZ. So, while your nephew was struggling to stay afloat in arctic waters, you thought: I'll have that baby penguin?

STITCH. It does seem wrong. When you put it like that.

LIZ. And now what?

STITCH. What d'you mean?

LIZ. Well, what are you planning to do now?

Pause.

STITCH. I suppose I haven't, completely thought it through.

Mostly just been racking my brains how to smuggle it out again without you noticing.

MARK. Any thoughts?

STITCH, *forlorn, shakes his head.*

Probably a bit late now anyway.

LIZ. This isn't funny, Mark.

MARK. I'm sorry but. There's a baby penguin in our bathroom.

LIZ. Exactly.

MARK *and* LIZ *stare at each other,* LIZ *frowning,* MARK *smiling. It is a battle of wills. Gradually, and with regret,* MARK's *smile fades.*

MARK. I'll give Dave a ring.

STITCH. Oh, Mark, no. Please. He already thinks I'm odd.

MARK. Don't worry, he loves all this. Freaks and that. Sort of collects them.

STITCH. That isn't very comforting, Mark.

MARK. Fine, I'll tell him it was Sam.

LIZ. You will not.

MARK. Can't do any harm. And look at him. Distressed. Knitting.

STITCH *looks distressed, and starts knitting.*

LIZ. And what about poor Sam? Just getting the feeling back in his toes after what by all accounts has been a bit of a traumatic afternoon, the police come round, his uncle's blaming him for –

MARK. Come on, Liz, I hardly think the police'll be round.

LIZ (*raising her voice*). He nicked. A penguin.

Silence.

STITCH. Not on purpose.

LIZ. Leave it out, Stitch. (*To* MARK.) Just ring him, alright?

MARK (*picking up phone*). I'll um. I'll go through there.

MARK *and the phone go offstage.* LIZ, *still angry, sits down heavily, plugs some headphones into the CD player, changes CD, presses play. She puts the headphones on either side of the bump. Sighs.* STITCH, *who is knitting with one eye on* LIZ, *pauses.*

STITCH. How's the bump?

LIZ. Been better. (*Pause.*) Gets worked up, so, the health visitor said play it some music. Tried everything really: Morrissey, whale song, Girls Aloud. Only thing that works is Kate Bush.

STITCH. I love Kate Bush.

LIZ (*still cross*). It's your CD. So. You've got something right. (*Sighs.*) I shouldn't've… I'm just. I'm not mad. I'm disappointed.

STITCH (*smiling*). You'll be a really good mum.

LIZ (*still cross*). Yeah, I know.

(*Softening.*) Can't wait, to be honest. All that breast-feeding. Nappies. Special parking spaces at Asda. Brilliant. No need to turn up on time for anything ever again. Just wander round looking washed-out, finishing off everyone's Happy Meals and catching sick in the pockets of my jeans. Funny really,

I've looked at Lauren all this time, with Sam. And I know fourteen was a bit young but. I'm glad I'm catching up. Part of it. Motherhood. Just feels right, somehow.

STITCH. Yeah?

LIZ. You wouldn't understand. Not sure Mark does. Still. Worth a try.

STITCH *looks hurt*.

(*Stroking bump*.) Gone to sleep.

MARK *comes back in*.

MARK. Dave's popping round when he finishes. Says he won't be long.

LIZ. Cheers.

MARK. No trouble.

STITCH. I think I might clear off for a bit. See how Sam's doing. (*Picking up lunchbox*.) Take him this back.

MARK. Sure?

STITCH. Yeah. Might be a bit awkward otherwise. You know, already seen Dave once today. Don't want to run out of things to talk about. So early on.

MARK (*laughs*). No. That is a worry.

STITCH. I'll just pop in and. Say my goodbyes.

STITCH *ducks into the bathroom and closes the door.*
MARK *sits next to LIZ on the sofa and sighs.*

Fade.

Scene Two

LIZ *is sitting on the sofa, flicking through a magazine.* MARK *is curled up next to her with his head on the bump, eating the Battenberg.* LIZ *strokes his hair, gently.*

MARK. Do you think fetuses ever wank?

LIZ (*she cuffs him*). No.

MARK. Alright.

> MARK *offers* LIZ *a bite of the Battenberg, wafting it in front of her face. She turns her nose up. He goes back to eating it himself. She smiles, strokes his hair again. Then frowns.*

LIZ. You have thought about the bump and that, haven't you? What it means.

MARK. Yeah, course I have.

LIZ. Really?

MARK. Really. I need a proper job, which I've got. Sort of. Start sterilising stuff. Stop sleeping. Can't be that hard if your sister would rather do it than her GCSEs. Only thing she ever passed, that pregnancy test.

LIZ. I'm serious, Mark. Big changes. Are you ready for all that?

MARK (*sighs*). Is this about the sofa?

LIZ. I'm just not sure I can bring up a child with a man who is so reluctant to get a new sofa.

MARK. Always comes back to this.

LIZ. Well, you keep digging your heels in.

MARK. So do you.

LIZ. Because it's hideous.

Silence.

MARK. Harsh, Liz. Brutal.

LIZ. Look at it. Tatty, mucky, frayed.

MARK. I do look at it, Liz. I look at it, and I see: a friend.

LIZ *sighs, exasperated.*

I know we only got it to see us through till we could find
something better. I remember. I was there. But honestly, all
those ones at IKEA – the Karlstad, the Ektorp, the Tylösand
with the contrasting Klippan footstools – they didn't come
close, not even close to this one.

LIZ. Mark.

MARK. No, Liz. I mean it. I've never encountered such a loyal
piece of furniture. It's comfy. Supportive. Always there when
I get home from work. Even in the bad times, the IKEA
days, it never judged, never once said: traitor; hypocrite. And
now, I admit: I'm attached. I shouldn't be, but I am. And –
(*Moved.*) I won't let you just cast it out, like.

LIZ. Like my brother.

MARK. No.

LIZ. Mark, you're being a knob.

MARK. I'm standing my ground.

LIZ. Well, don't. You're about to be a dad. You need to think
about your priorities. Nothing will ever be the same again.

Beat.

MARK. The sofa will.

LIZ. I can't believe you're being so stubborn. On top of everything else today. Sam could've drowned, there's a penguin in
the shower tray, I'm dying for the loo, my blood pressure's
rocketing, the bump's staying put, my ankles have swollen
up to the size they were before Paul McKenna made me thin,
and I'm just. I dunno. I'm dead worried about Stitch.

MARK (*quietly*). Why?

LIZ. What d'you mean, why?

MARK. I just meant, apart from, you know. He seems alright.

LIZ. You don't think he's been a bit down?

MARK. No more than usual. Bound to be a bit underwhelmed, all that time selling wool.

LIZ. Not just wool.

MARK. No, but. Mostly.

LIZ. There's silks, ribbon, knitting patterns. All manner of ginghams.

MARK. You're right, it's handicraft heaven. Everything a young gay man could wish for. The things he could crochet.

Pause.

LIZ. I found something in his bag.

MARK. You went through his stuff?

LIZ. I was looking for Battenberg.

MARK. Think you're the one we need to be worried about.

LIZ. It's the bump. It loves it.

MARK (*smiling*). Handy, that is.

LIZ. Hang on.

LIZ *rummages in the bag, finds a bottle of pills and hands them to* MARK.

See.

MARK (*nods*). I thought his hair looked glossy.

LIZ. What?

MARK. Kelp.

LIZ. Oh. Wrong ones, um.

She finds another bottle and shows them to MARK.

Here.

MARK. Oh.

That's never a good sign, is it?

Still. He'll be fine with Sam till we've sorted out the bathroom situation. And I'll drop him home tomorrow. Your mum'll know what's best.

LIZ. You think?

MARK. Positive.

He's been a bit weird with Dave too, apparently.

LIZ. How d'you mean?

MARK. Nothing bad, just. Clingy. Rung him a couple of times, I dunno. Turned up at work.

LIZ. That's nice.

MARK. Dave doesn't really do all that, so much.

LIZ. What does he do?

MARK. LSD, I think. Mostly.

LIZ. Sounds like a brilliant match, Mark. Well done.

MARK. I'm sorry. I didn't think they'd.

Knock on the door.

Speak of the devil.

Fade.

Scene Three

DAVE *has arrived. He is still dressed as a giant penguin. He and* LIZ *are obviously unimpressed with one another, looking away even when talking.* MARK *seems painfully aware of the awkwardness.*

MARK. Liz, this is Dave. Dave, my wife, Liz.

DAVE. Alright.

   Beat.

LIZ. See you've dressed the part.

DAVE (*nods, humourless*). Thought it'd be a laugh. (*Nobody laughs.*) You're pregnant, then.

LIZ. Yeah.

DAVE. Who's the dad?

   Beat.

LIZ. Mark is.

DAVE. Ooh, unlucky, mate. Gutted. Still. Never too late for adoption.

MARK. Oh, I hardly think –

DAVE. Seriously, tell them you're on smack, they sort it out, no questions. Sister does it all the time. Though. She is actually on smack, so.

LIZ. Well, Mark's pleased to be having the baby. Thrilled. Aren't you?

MARK. Oh, thrilled, yeah.

LIZ. See? Thrilled.

DAVE. Mm. Thrilled. (*Pause.*) You've changed your tune.

MARK. Yeah, well. You do, when –

DAVE. I remember when –

MARK. Oh mate, don't.

DAVE. Relax. I'm just going to tell Liz about –

MARK. I wouldn't bother, it'll just –

LIZ. What?

DAVE. Just a funny story.

MARK. Not funny.

DAVE. Funny-ish.

MARK. Liz, honestly. Borderline dull –

LIZ. Stop interrupting. Come on, Dave. Spit it out.

DAVE. Just, down the pub one night, right. Family come in. Kids everywhere, drinking Coke, smacking each other with pool cues, the lot. He said to me: Dave, I'm not gay.

LIZ. Good start.

MARK. Leave it, Dave, please.

DAVE. He said: I'm not gay, but.

MARK. Don't feel you two have to, sort of, bond, we can just get the –

DAVE. He said to me: Dave, I'm not gay, but it'd almost be worth it to make sure I never ended up like that poor sod.

MARK. Love, I –

DAVE. I cannot imagine, he said.

LIZ. Oh, more, brilliant.

DAVE. He said: I cannot imagine anything worse, on this earth, than having kids.

MARK. It was a long, long time ago, Liz –

DAVE (*laughing*). Thank God, he said, they're starting to think Liz is infertile.

Silence.

Funny how things turn out.

LIZ. Yeah.

MARK. It was ages ago, Liz. I've –

LIZ. How long ago?

MARK. Oh, too long to –

DAVE. About nine months, I'd say. Ish. (*Sizing* LIZ *up.*) So. When's it due?

LIZ *and* MARK *look at each other. Both seem wounded.* DAVE *raises an imaginary glass.*

Fatherhood.

And sits down. Silence. MARK *is close to tears.*

Cracking sofa, this, you've done well.

Silence. LIZ *looks like this is the last straw.*

(*Sighs.*) Nice as this is: had I better see about the penguin? Before thingy gets back. Eh, mate – you were right about him. Worst yet, I reckon. Still, blowjob's a blowjob, I suppose. Can't complain. Technique was a bit left field, but.

LIZ. That's my brother you're talking about.

DAVE. And it's his fault my job's on the line, so. I'll say it how I see it. Can't be doing with all this tiptoeing on eggshells whenever someone's a bit mental.

MARK. We are sorry. About the penguin and that.

DAVE. Happens all the time.

LIZ (*doubtful*). Really?

DAVE. Yeah. Something about aquariums just draws the nutters in. I reckon it's the sharks.

LIZ. Stitch isn't a nutter.

DAVE. Ooh, definite screw loose.

MARK. He did nick a penguin, Liz.

LIZ. He's dyslexic.

DAVE. How did he get it out, that's what I want to know. How did he do it?

MARK. Just shoved it in Sam's pack-up box, he said.

DAVE. Can I –

MARK. Taken it back to Sam, as it happens. Hope he washed it. What's funny?

DAVE. Nowt really, just. The fuss we have moving them round, about eight of us to catch one, sedate it, special crate thing to put them in for safe transport – got one with me in the van. Right sodding circus. And he just pops one in a Tupperware tub and wanders home.

MARK. S'pose it is quite odd.

DAVE. Wouldn't do it twice, I tell you that for nothing.

MARK. I bet.

DAVE. No way. No bloody way.

MARK. Mm.

Silence. Gradually it dawns on MARK *and* LIZ *what has happened.* MARK *first.*

Shit.

DAVE. What?

MARK. Shit, shit, shit.

MARK *goes into the bathroom, looks for the penguin, finds nothing. Comes back in, empty-handed.*

LIZ (*managing not to laugh*). Shit.

DAVE. What?

MARK. He's done it again. Stitch. It's gone.

DAVE. What? Oh, frigging. Nutter. What did I tell you?
Mentalist. I'm gonna be frigging unemployed, it's not even a
joke. You are kidding. You are kidding me. You are having
me on.

MARK *shakes his head.* DAVE *kicks the sofa in annoyance.*

LIZ (*standing up slowly*). In that case, gentlemen: think I'll just
nip to the loo.

LIZ, *with a hint of triumph, goes into the bathroom.*

Fade.

Scene Four

MARK *is talking on the phone.* DAVE *is sat listening, still
looking furious.*

MARK. Cheers then, Sam, bye. (*Puts the phone down.*) He's
not been there.

DAVE. I need that penguin back, Mark.

MARK. I know you do.

DAVE. Seriously, though. I'm in trouble as it is with the kid
falling in. Left the birds in a right state. To be fair, I said, at
least it moved the crowd on from that jellyfish with a fungal
infection. Looks like Mick Hucknall. But they were all:
should've jumped in after the boy, it looks bad. Big talk. But
you don't know if you'll sink or swim in one of these, do
you? Anyway, nutter-boy dragged him out in the end.
Wouldn't think he had it in him.

MARK. No.

DAVE. Where will he be then? Think.

MARK. Not a clue. Could be anywhere.

DAVE. Got a car?

MARK. No. Fast runner, though.

DAVE. And there's buses.

MARK. Oh yeah, course.

DAVE. We'll have to find him. What if we leave wifey here in case he comes back, then split up or something?

MARK. Like in a film?

DAVE. S'pose.

Pause.

MARK. Nah. I can't leave Liz on her own.

DAVE. Bloody hell, Mark.

MARK. What?

DAVE. She's a big girl.

MARK. Exactly.

DAVE. Massive.

MARK. That's it: she could, you know. Any minute really. And she's had a curry.

DAVE *sighs.*

What?

DAVE. Nothing, just. Inconvenient, isn't it?

Bathroom door opens a crack.

Do you not realise, this is the life you're choosing? Stuck with some stroppy woman, all the time giving birth.

MARK. I hardly think –

LIZ (*a worried, small voice*). Mark.

MARK (*turns round*). What's up, love?

LIZ. I think I've started.

DAVE. Oh, frigging hell.

MARK. Oh. Oh Liz. Come on out. Sit down a minute, I'll. Come on, come on out.

LIZ. Ring us a taxi, will you?

MARK. What?

LIZ. And the hospital.

MARK. What're you on about?

LIZ. Just do it, will you?

MARK. But. I'm taking you in.

LIZ. If you don't want it.

MARK. Course I want it.

LIZ. Doesn't sound like it.

MARK. Course I do.

LIZ. I'll do it on my own. You can just –

MARK. Liz, seriously, come out now.

LIZ. No, Mark, I mean it. I am an independent woman. A survivor. I'm practically Beyoncé.

MARK. Love, I know.

LIZ. Well, if you think I need you to do this, with your stupid pub chat and your shitty mates, you're wrong. Your bit's done, spermy. You can just go.

MARK. Liz.

LIZ. Lauren did it by herself. And I've got GCSEs. Geography, Art, Dual Award Science. What have you got to bring to the table?

Pause.

MARK. Textiles?

LIZ. Exactly. You give Stitch a hard time about knitting, never let on we've got a cupboard full of napkins you embroidered with important scenes from the Bayeux Tapestry. Not so hard in front of your penguin mate now, are you?

MARK. Suppose not.

LIZ. No. Good.

Pause.

MARK (*calmly*). I wonder, though: is now the best time to be having this conversation? Just come out, love, please. I'll get the bag. Think about breathing and that. In and out.

LIZ. Yes, I know how to bloody breathe.

MARK. Alright.

LIZ *comes out of the bathroom and leans against the arm of the sofa with her back to* DAVE, *who is sulking.* MARK *goes offstage to get the hospital bag.* LIZ *and* DAVE *remain silent for a while, then:*

DAVE. Typical.

LIZ. Right, that's it: Mark, I've changed my mind.

MARK *reappears.*

MARK. Sorry, missed that.

LIZ. I've changed my mind.

MARK. What?

LIZ. I'm stopping here till I know Stitch is safe.

MARK. Liz –

LIZ. I'll be fine. Cross my legs, I'll be ages yet. I'm not leaving him in charge.

MARK. Liz, it's not safe. You need doctors and.

LIZ. They'll only put me in a room for the first few hours. I'll have to sit through bloody, *Flashdance* or something.

MARK. You love *Flashdance*.

LIZ. I meant *Rambo*. Anyway – (*Still with her back to* DAVE.) worst comes to the worst, he'll know what to do. Works in a zoo.

DAVE. Aquarium actually, but.

LIZ. Penguins still give birth.

DAVE. Think you'll find they hatch, actually, so.

MARK. It's true, love. They do hatch.

LIZ. Oh, David Attenborough: sod off. (*Grabbing stomach*.) *Christ*, that was weird.

MARK. What's up?

LIZ. Well, I'm not hatching, am I?

MARK. Sorry.

DAVE (*to himself*). That doesn't even make sense.

LIZ. It's no good, we'll have to go. Are you in or not?

MARK. Course I'm in. Course I am. (*Kisses* LIZ*'s head*.) Don't be daft.

LIZ. Right then.

MARK. Brilliant, I'll just.

    MARK *leaves to get the bag again*.

LIZ (*still with her back to* DAVE). You'll wait here for Stitch?

DAVE (*sulking*). No choice now, really, is there?

LIZ. And ring Mark when he gets back? On his mobile? Leave a voicemail if he's not answering?

DAVE. S'pose.

LIZ. Well, will you or not?

DAVE. Might as well.

LIZ. And at least be, I dunno. Civil, to him?

DAVE. Always civil, aren't I? God. (*Under his breath.*) Bitch.

MARK *returns with bag.*

MARK. Right. Everybody alright? Dave? Liz? Brilliant.
(*Touching* LIZ *lightly on the arm, but talking to* DAVE.) If
there's, you know. Keep in touch. Make yourself at home
and that.

DAVE. Love to. Cheers.

MARK (*a little bit exhilarated*). Right then. Right. Cracking.
Let's go, um. Let's go have a baby.

MARK *and* LIZ *leave.*

Fade.

ACT THREE

Unravelling

'Most problems are eventually overcome with patience, hard work and skill – a difficult sleeve, collar or buttonhole needn't spell disaster. Sometimes, though, the only way forward is by unravelling. Do it quickly and without regret, taking comfort in the knowledge that, while all your work has amounted to very little so far, at least you haven't wasted good wool.'

A Girl's Guide to Knitting & Crochet, Janice Thripp (1962)

Scene One

*Night has fallen, and the room is lit dimly by a small lamp.
DAVE sits alone on the sofa, snoozing. He wakes up, picks the
Battenberg up, nibbles a bit, pulls a face, and puts it down.
Fidgets. Starts to nod off again, as STITCH comes in quietly, and
sits down, embarrassed. DAVE jerks awake and seems annoyed.*

DAVE. Look who's back.

STITCH. Hiya.

DAVE. Where've you been?

STITCH. Jackson's.

> STITCH *takes a bottle of vodka out of his pocket and offers
> it to* DAVE, *who pushes it away.*

DAVE. For four hours.

STITCH. Had a walk as well. You're not meant to. Not safe.
But it's quite nice, really, Hull at night. Can't see it so much.

> DAVE *is dialling* MARK*'s number.*

DAVE. And the penguin?

> STITCH *shrugs. Hugs the lunchbox close to his chest.*

> Mark, mate, it's me. He's back. Yeah. Pissed. Won't say. You
> alright? Right. Ooh. Right. See you.

STITCH. Where's Mark?

DAVE. Hospital. With Liz.

STITCH. Oh.

> *Pause.* DAVE *waits.*

> Oh shit, is she – she alright?

DAVE. Mark says she's fine. Mouth like a sewer but. You know: on her way.

STITCH. Thank God.

DAVE. Seriously, mate, the penguin?

Reluctantly, STITCH *opens the lunchbox.*

Fuck.

Pause. They both sit looking into the box.

STITCH. Um. It's dead.

DAVE. I can see that.

STITCH. Alright.

DAVE. What happened?

STITCH. Nothing. It just died.

DAVE. You absolute pillock.

STITCH. What'll you do?

DAVE. Nothing I can do now, is there? Sneak it back in with the others. Say it died there. You're off the frigging hook.

STITCH. Cheers.

DAVE. Not doing it for you, am I? For my job.

STITCH. Oh.

DAVE. I think it's savage, what you've done. I don't think there's a sight in this world more pathetic than a dead penguin. And what's that round its neck? Some sick little costume. A little bonnet you've knitted? Scarf?

STITCH (*upset*). It's a snood.

DAVE *looks at him in disbelief.*

Quite a chilly night. Thought it might be cold.

DAVE. It's a frigging penguin. As if killing it wasn't enough. You should be locked up.

STITCH. There's nothing wrong with snoods.

DAVE. It's you there's something wrong with. Mark was right. Frigging useless.

Why d'you take it in the first place?

STITCH *shrugs*.

Come on. Why?

STITCH. Dunno. Just. This afternoon. I thought you'd be pleased to see me. And then. It threw me. A bit.

DAVE. Why would I be pleased to see you?

STITCH. Cos we…

DAVE *laughs*.

I don't –

DAVE. It doesn't mean anything.

STITCH. But you said.

DAVE. It doesn't matter what I said, mate. Can't even remember. I left it behind the wheelie bin with the johnny and that lingering sense of disappointment. Oh, whatever. I know what you were after: poetry and that. No doubt love came into it. Some cosy little boyfriend to go with your knitting and your frigging, Battenberg. Well, it doesn't work like that, mate. Not round here. And, you know. Definitely not with me.

STITCH. What about the penguins and that?

DAVE. We're not penguins.

STITCH *gives* DAVE *a look that takes in his costume, but doesn't say anything*.

Just some shit I heard on the radio. What? Seriously, mate. Listen up: you are nothing more to me than a kooky shag.

Pause.

STITCH (*hurt*). Kooky?

DAVE. Very kooky. And, if I'm honest, not even a shag.
Worried noises in a tank top. I'd've been better off sticking
with Venereal Phil. At least you've got something to show
for your night out.

STITCH. That's a horrible thing to say.

DAVE. How would you know? I've pulled some decent lads at
that clinic. James: fit as. Got chatting by one of them little
stands they have full of leaflets about herpes. We'd've done
it then if he hadn't picked one up. You, though. Don't know
what to make of you.

Pause.

STITCH (*at this point, utterly broken*). Was it. The humming?

*Silence. DAVE looks exasperated, embarrassed to be there.
STITCH starts to hum the introduction to 'Funky Town'.
Stops. Starts again.*

DAVE. Would you stop it?

STITCH (*as much to himself as anything*). I'm just. I was just.
Nervous. And it was taking so long.

DAVE. No wonder.

STITCH. I thought it'd be over quick.

DAVE. What are you –

STITCH. Like a Mini Milk, sort of three good licks and a joke
at the end but. No.

DAVE. Thank God.

STITCH. If anything: Calippo. You know how your mouth gets
numb and, and the wrapper goes all soggy round the edges.

DAVE. Enough.

STITCH. And then the juice.

DAVE. Why are you telling me this?

STITCH (*upset*). I don't know. Helps to. Get things off your chest a bit. Sometimes.

DAVE. Right. I'll take this and. Don't suppose I'll be seeing you again.

STITCH. No.

DAVE. Will the kid want his box back?

STITCH (*sadly*). I'll get him a new one. Probably smells a bit of. Death and that.

DAVE. I'm off then.

STITCH (*looking down*). Right.

DAVE. Right.

STITCH. See you then.

DAVE. Yeah.

STITCH. Right.

> DAVE *doesn't go*. STITCH *doesn't look up*.

DAVE. I wondered, though.

STITCH. Sorry?

DAVE. If you fancied…

STITCH. I don't –

DAVE. You know. Another crack, at it.

STITCH. Pardon?

DAVE. You heard. I figured, we're both here now. Long night. Flat to ourselves. Bit of practice won't hurt you. And I'll take one for the team.

> DAVE *is lightly stroking the crotch of the penguin suit*.

STITCH. Think I'll pass, thanks.

DAVE. What?

STITCH. Think I've probably had enough. For one day.

DAVE. You can't say no to life for ever, mate.

STITCH. I can tonight.

DAVE. Pathetic. You know that? Pathetic.

DAVE *exits, annoyed.* STITCH *takes the headphones out of the CD player and presses play. As Kate Bush sings 'This Woman's Work', he drinks with a blank face. Cries gently. As the song draws to a close, he reaches into his bag, finds a bottle of pills and stands them on the table next to the vodka.*

Fade.

Scene Two

Darkness. STITCH*'s silhouette is just visible, unconscious on the sofa. A few moments' silence, then the phone begins to ring.* STITCH *doesn't stir. It rings for a bit then clicks onto the answer machine.*

ANSWERPHONE. Hello?

MARK. Stitch, that you?

ANSWERPHONE. Just kidding. Liz and Mark are out, leave us a message. Beep.

MARK. Bloody thing. Stitch, it's Mark. Just to say, you're an uncle. Again. Liz is fine, knackered, and the bump's out. We're calling it Emma. It's a girl. You must be asleep, so. I'll see you in the morning. Good news, though, eh?

ANSWERPHONE *clicks off.*

Fade.

Scene Three

Day. MARK *is cleaning the sofa with soapy water and a cloth. He stops, examines the cushion, puts it down. Puts down the cloth. Breathes out and puts his head in his hands for a few moments of complete despair.*

STITCH *comes in from the bathroom, with his toothbrush and toothpaste, hurries over to* MARK.

STITCH. What's up?

MARK. Nothing, just. (*Sighs.*) I'm shit at clearing up sick. Sort of makes me gag.

STITCH. Oh Mark, you shouldn't be doing that.

MARK. It's fine.

STITCH. No, let me.

STITCH *takes the cloth, kneels by the sofa and starts wiping the cushions.*

MARK. If you're not up to it.

STITCH. I'm fine.

MARK. Sure?

STITCH. Honestly. Thank you, but.

Pause. MARK *sits on the arm of the sofa and watches* STITCH, *wondering how to approach talking about the night before. The best he can come up with is:*

MARK. So. Been a bit down?

STITCH. Bit down, yeah.

Pause. More cleaning.

MARK. Can't believe you overdosed on kelp.

You'll have such strong nails.

STITCH. Bonus.

Pause. Cleaning.

MARK. Why d'you do it, Stitch?

STITCH. Got the wrong pills.

MARK. No, I meant.

STITCH. Oh. You know. This and that.

Pause.

MARK. Tricky stain?

STITCH. Yeah.

MARK. I couldn't shift it.

STITCH. Have you got any Vanish Mousse?

MARK. Erm. Not that I know of.

STITCH. Flash Spray?

MARK *shakes his head*. STITCH *sniffs the sofa cushion*.

Febreze might help.

MARK. Don't think so.

STITCH. Oust?

MARK. Stitch, you're obviously upset.

STITCH. I just need cleaning products.

MARK (*softening*). Leave it for now, eh? I'll pick something up later, and.

STITCH. No. I want to sort it before I go. Liz might be home tonight, and Emma.

MARK. Don't know why you've got it into your head you have to go.

STITCH *doesn't say anything*.

Liz'll be upset if she's missed you. And you've got to wait and see Emma.

STITCH. I'll see them another time.

MARK. Not the same, though, is it?

STITCH *shrugs*.

Stitch, you'll have to talk to me. I don't understand what's.

STITCH. I had a good think last night. While I was projectile vomiting. And I decided, perhaps the gay scene of Hull isn't for me. It's the vodka, I think. Among other things. Honestly. I looked deep inside myself. And I just found: wool. I'm not a great one for nightclubs, not a party animal. Can't imagine I ever will be. I don't even like sex that much, to be honest. Rather have a good yoghurt. I think the best thing I can hope to do with my life is. Knitting.

MARK. You don't have to –

STITCH. It's alright. I like hanging round with old ladies in experimental cardigans. They're nice. Kind. I fit in. Think they've even twigged about, you know. Always speak very highly of Dale Winton when I'm around, so. Perhaps I'd better just. Do that. For a bit.

Pause.

MARK. Well, I'm not convinced. I thought you wanted to be away from all that.

STITCH. I did. Sort of. Just. I'm not sure I'm. There's days when you feel so buoyant and. Capable. Then something'll just. I dunno. And you're. Overwhelmed this. Sadness. Do you not hear it sometimes? Behind things, everything really, this, I dunno. This sad heart beating.

Pause.

MARK (*dreading the answer*). Have you done it before?

STITCH. Not really.

I thought about it once, but, you know. Nothing came of it.

MARK. When was this?

STITCH. Back home. November-ish. Silly really.

Took myself down to the beach one afternoon. Sat in the shingle, looking for fossils. Didn't find much. Half a devil's toenail. Bit off an ammonite's shell. A tampon. Then I watched the waves for a bit. They've got a rhythm, you know. Sort of: inviting. I thought: I could just keep sitting here, let it wash round me, like arms. No one'd know. Then I thought: actually. Looks a bit cold. Went home and watched *Countdown*. It's not the same without Carol Vorderman but still. Better than. You know.

MARK. Oh, absolutely. Much better, no question. No question about that. (*Pause.*) No question.

STITCH. Alright.

MARK *notices* STITCH *is crying.*

MARK. Oh God, Stitch, just. (*Guiding* STITCH *onto the sofa next to him.*) Sit up here a minute. Hey. (*Puts an arm round him, a bit stiffly.*) Ssh. Hey. Come on. What's up?

STITCH (*quietly, but not crying any more*). I'm in the wet patch.

MARK. Shit, sorry I. Didn't think.

MARK *moves onto the arm,* STITCH *to the dry side of the sofa.*

Sorry.

STITCH. It's fine, I'm sorry. You've just had a baby.

MARK. Not me personally.

STITCH (*getting upset again*). No, but, you don't need all this from some tit who nicked a penguin then tried to top himself.

MARK. Hey.

STITCH. I'm sorry, I –

MARK. Hey. Ssh.

STITCH. I'm so glad you're here.

MARK. Yeah, well, you know. I'm glad you're here.

STITCH. But I mean, I shouldn't be –

MARK. Come on, Stitch. Calm down. Just, tell me what's up.

STITCH (*calming down again*). Oh, I dunno. I'm just so. (*Deep breath.*) Embarrassed.

MARK (*smiles*). Well, there's no need for that for a start. You've not done anything wrong. Listen, if there's one thing I learned when I was working at IKEA: things fall apart.

STITCH *smiles*.

For no reason sometimes. Happens to everyone. Honestly.

STITCH. Yeah?

MARK. Course it does. Before I met your sister, I was in a right state. No job, not eating properly, drinking far too much. We don't really talk about it now, but: I had a mullet. Spent eight months shut up by myself doing a four-foot embroidered portrait of Meat Loaf.

STITCH (*surprised*). That one in the airing cupboard?

MARK *looks more surprised*.

I tried hiding the penguin in there.

MARK (*looking down*). Oh.

STITCH. You made that?

MARK. I'm not proud.

Pause.

STITCH. I didn't know you were into… Meat Loaf and that.

MARK (*smiles*). Not so much these days.

STITCH. But, I mean. It's beautiful.

MARK (*touched*). Oh. Cheers.

STITCH. Bit dark, but.

MARK. It was a dark time for me, if I'm honest. Lonely.

STITCH. What happened?

MARK. Oh, it's. It's boring really. Just, you know. Heartbreak. Lies. All the classics.

STITCH *looks sad*. MARK *sighs*.

Alright. (*Deep breath.*)

Her name was Lola. She was a showgirl.

STITCH (*smiling*). Not sure I believe that, Mark.

MARK. Fine, her name was Lisa. Worked in Superdrug. Not as funny.

STITCH. You don't have to make it funny.

MARK. I know, just. What you do, isn't it? Take the worst of your life, turn it round. Laugh at it. Cos it can't do any harm, can it? No one ever died of a joke.

STITCH. Suppose.

MARK. Kelp, on the other hand. Lethal.

STITCH (*smiling*). Alright.

MARK. You should try it, though. I mean. Just a thought. Stay here and we'll help.

STITCH. Help laugh at me?

MARK. Yeah.

STITCH. It's a kind offer, Mark.

MARK. Well: I'm all heart.

Eh, are you wavering?

STITCH (*smiles*). Might be.

MARK. Nice one.

I really think it could work. You'd be happy here and that.

Pause. STITCH *thinks about staying here or returning home. He makes his decision, and sticks to it with a new touch of firmness in his voice.*

STITCH. No, it's.

MARK. What?

STITCH. I just think, it's a bit more complicated than –

MARK. You're making excuses now.

STITCH. No. You and Liz and Emma need time together. All that bonding and that. It's important.

MARK. You need to bond too.

STITCH. I will, just. Not yet. State I'm in.

It's so kind of you, honestly, but. I'm ready to go back, really. (*Brave face.*) To Withernsea. It's you they need, Mark.

MARK. Don't say that.

STITCH. It is.

MARK. Doubt I've got it in me.

STITCH. You do, though.

MARK. Stitch, I'm not kidding. I stood there last night watching it all and. I dunno. I mean: I said all the right things and that. Ooh, look at her little fingers, her little toes. Thank God they're not webbed.

STITCH. See?

MARK. This is it, though: there I was, holding her for the first time, heartbeat to heartbeat, the most precious thing I've ever touched. So delicate. Perfect, really. And all I kept thinking in the back of my mind was: I'm still not getting rid of that sofa.

Now this.

They both look at the sofa for a bit.

STITCH. Perhaps a throw might help?

Pause. MARK *sighs, decision made. He borrows the quiet firmness in his voice from* STITCH, *like he's trying it out. It seems to work.*

MARK. No, I.

You wouldn't give us a hand?

STITCH. What d'you mean?

MARK. Get it outside.

STITCH *looks surprised.*

That's the rules. If you go, so does…

STITCH. Oh Mark.

MARK. No, it's good. Fresh start. For Liz and that.

STITCH. Are you sure?

MARK. Think so. Think she'd like that. She was fairly clear.

STITCH (*smiles*). Well. I mean. If you're positive, then.

Pause. MARK *strokes the sofa tenderly.*

MARK. Right. Right then. Let's have it outside.

They carry the sofa offstage.

Fade.

ABOUT A GOTH

About A Goth was first performed by Owen Whitelaw at Òran Mór, Glasgow, on 28 September 2009, directed by Tessa Walker.

NICK, *a goth, seventeen.*

As beds go it is passable, I suppose. Obviously I would prefer to sleep in a coffin but as my mum has so hilariously pointed out, they don't sell coffins at IKEA.
Yet.
I've written a letter informing the managing director about this potentially profitable gap in the market. I also included some of my own designs, though I'm not particularly hopeful about the whole thing. Partly because all hope is futile, and partly because I doubt they even have goths in Sweden. Just Vikings and that. Ulrika Jonsson.
I check my phone but. Nothing. Greg still hasn't replied to my text. It has been three days and eleven hours now, which seems a bit relaxed even for someone as simple as him. Look in my sent messages. It's there in capital letters:
I HATE MYSELF AND I WANT TO DIE.
I wonder if I've been too subtle again. Probably. I forget not everyone is as emotionally mature and sensitive as me. I decide to have a wank, but even that is doomed. Halfway through, I start worrying about getting stains on my new black duvet cover. My heart isn't in it after that. Four out of ten, probably. If only my jizz was as dark as my soul. It isn't though. That'd be impossible.

Breakfast is depressing as usual. All I want is to read Camus and eat my Coco Pops, but it is so hard to concentrate with Dad's armour clanking and Mum clattering about with her tankards in the sink. And they're always talking to me.
'Good day, young squire,' Mum says.
Dad gives me a kiss on the top of my head then goes back to jousting with a Swiss roll. Honestly. It's tragic. Everyone else's parents lie and cheat and have inner turmoil and chuck teapots at each other. I get the world's most cheerful medieval re-enactors. My mum leans over, dangles her fluted sleeve in my

chocolatey milk, passes me a postcard. It's got a donkey on the front. Looking jaunty.
'Camping is amazing.'
Three exclamation marks.
'Weather perfect.'
A further two exclamation marks.
'Dropped my phone off a cliff to prove it is shatterproof. It's not. That was my old phone. Brilliant.'
Underlined.
'Bet your missing me.'
'Your' spelt wrong.
'You big gay.'
No comment.
'Greg.'
And a kiss.

Pause.

'Fancy finishing off this mead?'
Mum holds out a bottle.
I give her a long, stern look.
'Wench, I do not.'

The bus isn't due for another ten minutes so I undo one of my badges and self-harm for a bit. I don't draw blood cos my cloak is dry clean only but it helps pass the time. The bus stop smells of piss and regret. It's a very sunny day, the worst kind of weather for a goth, so I lurk in the shadows contemplating the great tragedies of my life. The burden of my intelligence, for example. Loneliness.
I am an only child.
Unless you count Lizzie, my sister, but I don't since she is so clearly a moron.
Right on cue, she drives past the bus stop. Like a twat. Beeps her horn. Like a twat. Stops and winds the window down. Like a twat.
'Alright, gorgeous,' she says.
I could vom.
'Need a lift into town?'
'No, you div, just like hanging round bus stops on my own.'

(Actually, that is partly true.)
I get in the car. She's listening to James Blunt. I try to hurl
myself into the oncoming traffic. We compromise with the
soundtrack to *Flashdance*, which she considers one of the great
achievements of the twentieth century. I tell her I'll pass that on
to Jean-Paul Sartre, he will be pleased. She laughs, but doesn't
know why she is laughing. Such is the emptiness of life.
I get dropped off at the mini-roundabout. There is a sense of
foreboding and quite a big Starbucks. I buy a Mint Frappuccino,
the most gothic of the available drinks, and finish it in the
cemetery next door. Sit on a big old weathered slab with worn
out letters and moss. I'm keeping half an eye out for other goths
but it's pretty dead to be honest. A few widows with flowers and
that. The odd nun. I've got a muffin too but I'm saving it till
afterwards. Give me something to live for. Cos looking round
me, the graves have never seemed more inviting. In the end,
though, it's time. I slurp the last minty dregs and head off for
another two hours of misery.

The first thing you notice is the heat. They have the heating on
all through summer and I have discovered that hot pensioners
have a very particular smell. It is one part talc, two parts decay.
A goth with less of a social conscience might turn back at this
point, but I breathe through my mouth and look for Carol. I find
her in the activities room, where several old people are being
underwhelmed by a well-meaning Christian and his Casio
keyboard. I walk in on a passionate rendition of Celine Dion's
'My Heart Will Go On'.
I don't dwell on it.
Think it must be somebody's birthday. There are balloons
dotted about, and Elsie has put her teeth in. Carol spots me and
flushes with relief at having an excuse to leave.
A haunting flute solo follows us up the stairs.

'Every night in my dreams, I see you. I feel you. That is how I
know you go on.'
Greg looks horrified. I can see his reflection in the mirror.
'Nick, what are you playing at?'
I'm stood in his bedroom by the stereo. I've got my back to him.

'Far across the distance and spaces between us you have come to show you go on.'

'Seriously, Nick. This is weird. This is, you know. Weird.'

There is genuine panic in his voice. Which I wasn't really expecting.

'Near,' I tell him, 'far, wherever you are I believe that the heart does go on.'

Decide to leave it there.

Silence.

Then he spots what I've got in my hand.

'Oh shit, sorry Nick. Thought you were, you know, about to. You know.'

'No.'

'Right. Course not. Shit. Hey. Good one.'

Greg lies back on his bed. Looks at the ceiling, relieved. Shuffles across a bit. His duvet cover is old and faded and covered in Thundercats. I sit on Lion-O's face.

'I just can't believe you own Céline Dion's *Greatest Hits*.'

'I normally hide it,' he says. 'Must've forgotten.'

'Hide it?'

'Yeah. In the wardrobe. Under my porn.'

I am stunned.

'You've got porn? No wonder you're not sticking to your revision timetable, Greg.'

He just shrugs.

'You do realise: those people – they're not in love.'

'That's not really the point. Anyway, it's the only time I get to see girls.'

I give him a sceptical look.

It is a crap excuse for somebody with a Saturday job at Lush.

'It's true, Nick. You don't know what it's like. Spend your life surrounded by girls, they all just love you and, no offence but they must know they're wasting their time. I'm sat here gagging for it, no one even notices.'

I give him a sort of reassuring pat.

'Loads of people have noticed.'

It doesn't help. If anything he looks more troubled.

Smoothes out a crease in Cheetara's inner thigh. His fingers
brush against my hand by accident. Pulls them back dead quick.
I think about his face in the mirror and that.
We finish our Capri-Suns in silence.

'Will you be my boyfriend?'
This strikes me as a bit forward, but she must be in her eighties
so time is of the essence. Glides gracefully down from above.
She's backlit by a skylight and looks sort of heavenly. Like the
late Thora Hird. Carol's pushed past but I'm not sure about
stairlift etiquette. I wait on the landing instead.
She grins, giggles, tries again:
'Will you be my toyboy? I've had my cataracts done.'
I decide to put a stop to this uncalled-for harassment.
'Actually, I'm gay.'
She looks hurt. Purses her lips. Tuts.
'You as well.'
The stairlift carries on inching towards me. Slow. Inevitable.
She's got a hardback romance and a Horlicks. I can hear the
theme to *Jaws* in my head. But it's alright. She goes past into
the shadows without a word.
Bitch.
I set off after Carol.
At the top of the stairs there's a window. A neat-looking man is
stood there, gazing out, still as anything. He's got his coat on, a
tweedy sort of hat and his suitcase on the floor by his feet. Very
slowly consults his watch. Goes back to looking out the
window.

'You'll like Rod, he's a real character.'
Carol's a bit out of breath. She knocks on Rod's door. The telly
is on full-blast.
'Alright if we come in, Rod?'
No answer. She goes in anyway.
'Nick's here to see you.'
'Who?'
'You remember I told you about Nick.'
I go in.

He looks at me.

'Not interested.'

'Don't say that, Rod.'

'What's he come as? Grim Reaper?'

Carol looks apologetic.

'I think it looks dead smart, Nick. Like the advert: Scottish Widows.'

Rod snorts.

'What does he want?'

'Well, he's brought you a muffin.'

(Not strictly true, but I don't really feel like explaining.)

'You just sit down there, Nick. He appreciates the company. Don't you, Rod.'

It isn't a question.

'I'll be downstairs anyway. If you need me, just – '

Carol points at the panic button round Rod's neck and leaves. The door shuts slowly behind her.

I look at Rod.

Rod looks at the telly.

I look at the telly. There's nothing else to look at anyway. No photos or plants or. It is *Murder, She Wrote*. I sit back in the chair, clutching my baked goods. Feels like I might've got away with it.

Rod turns to me.

Spit all down his chin.

'About this muffin,' he says.

With every mouthful my heart sinks a little bit. I'm starting to wonder if I'm really cut out for this. Voluntary work. I thought it'd be alright. And when I told people about it I got this deep, this sort of profound feeling of superiority which never quite happened with my paper round. But it's not like that really. It's more just watching shit telly with the BNP. I mean, I've got nothing against Angela Lansbury. As sleuths go. But Rod's seen each episode about a hundred times and it really gives him the upper hand when it comes to spotting the murderer.

'It'll be that Paki bastard.'

I look at him but bite my tongue.

'What?'

He says it lightly. Like a Nazi would.

'Nothing. Just, you know. What you just said: that is technically a hate crime.'

'Shut up, you. Frigging pansy.'

'As is that.'

Rod makes a noise. Like a choking sound. I lean over to check he's alright.

He is laughing. In my face.

A bit of muffin shoots out of his mouth and lands in the space between my eyebrows.

I stand up to go.

Didn't bloody come here for this. Bloody, abuse from pensioners. I'm meant to be bringing a ray of light to their dismal lives. Getting showered in Werther's Originals.

Unexpectedly included in a will, not gobbed on.

Get as far as the door and then stop.

Not because I want to. Not having second thoughts.

I'm just: stuck.

I hear Rod laugh. Feel a tug on my cloak. He is finding himself hilarious. I'm bloody not.

'Would you just let go?'

I hear that chokey gurgley sound again. Except this time it is me. The clasp bit is tight round my neck and I'm struggling to breathe. Start to panic a bit. Flap my arms. Try to pull myself free.

'Frigging, let go.'

He doesn't. I try to sort of throw myself forward. End up nutting the doorframe, which doesn't help.

'Get off, you twat.'

I'm really struggling to breathe now. Take a step back to loosen it but Rod just reels me in like a fish.

'GET OFF.'

'Or what?' Rod's still laughing.

'What're you going to do exactly?'

I try to keep my voice calm.

He obviously has no idea what I'm capable of.

'I should warn you: both my parents are medieval re-enactors.'

He pisses himself at that. Gives my cloak one last massive yank, pulls me backwards, right off balance.

The fabric rips a little bit. Just a little bit but.

That is it.

I turn on him quick as anything and, you know. It all goes sort of ninja.

Clang.

Whoosh.

Aargh.

Ow.

These are the sounds of war.

It is Friday 25th October, St Crispin's Day, in the year of our Lord, 1415. Just over there the battle of Agincourt is in full swing. Behind the ice-cream van. Near the pylon. I'm eight years old and feeling a bit bewildered. Uncle Dan is thirty-six, recently divorced, and surrounded by sympathetic yet buxom peasants. He can't believe his luck. Lizzie's eleven. At the moment she is teaching a small group of French casualties the dance routine to 'One for Sorrow' by Steps.

I'm worried about Mum and Dad.

I saw them leave about half an hour ago and noticed they were carrying quite a few weapons. They mentioned being hopelessly outnumbered by the French. My dad's got a dodgy hip, and Mum's a dinner lady. I think they might be out of their depth. I look at Lizzie but she's busy teaching a knight with a twisted ankle to grapevine. Uncle Dan is telling a passing minstrel about his eight-month struggle for custody. I try to get his attention but it's no good. The minstrel's got his lute out. Uncle Dan seems unconcerned but I sense there's a ballad in the offing and back slowly away. The noise from the battlefield gets louder.

Clang.

Whoosh.

Aargh.

Ow.

Pause.

I'll have to rescue them.

When the arrow hits me, I think I am going to die and I'm worried cos I still don't know if Mum and Dad are safe.

The archer is looking at me, a bit shaken. I pick the arrow up and wave at him to show I'm fine. I am so glad I wore a thick jumper, but when I look at the arrow it doesn't even have a point. Just a lump of heavy stuff, soft like plasticine. I feel a bit sorry for the archer. He won't kill many enemies like that.

I steal a dead man's shield to hide behind. No one tells me off so I carry on looking for Mum and Dad. It's so hard to see when everyone keeps charging about in front of me and swearing. Swords clash. Axes smack into helmets. It's all:

Clang.

Whoosh.

Aargh.

Ow.

Etcetera.

I'm feeling a bit anxious now.

Another arrow swooshes past my head. I duck behind my shield and in the corner of my eye, I think I see my dad. A man with a sword is smiting him down, like they do. I run over to see if it is my dad.

It's not my dad.

I am so relieved. I am so glad. I kick him but he's definitely dead.

A massive noise like a bugle or something but louder.

Everybody freezes.

People are shouting. People in fluorescent vests.

I am petrified.

All around me the dead people are standing up and shouting. And pointing. At me.

Hooves are pounding towards me. A massive horse is galloping at me. It is covered in a sort of blue-and-gold tablecloth thing, with holes for the eyes. A full suit of armour is riding the horse and I can't tell if there is someone inside or if it is a ghost. But I am more worried about the sword. And the hooves. And the dead people stood up around me, waving and that.

My heart is pounding like the hooves.

It is the only noise on the battlefield.

I sniff the air. It smells of fear and onions.

Mum is flipping livid. Dad is trying to calm her down. Uncle Dan has gone home in a huff.

I am just glad that everyone is safe.

'What were you thinking, Nicholas? You could've been...'

Nicholas. That is a bad sign. I feel myself go red.

'I was worried you and Dad might get hurt.'

'Nick,' Dad says. 'This is Agincourt. Only French people get hurt.'

I wish they'd told me that at the beginning.

After a bit everyone calms down. Mum apologises to Henry the Fifth for spoiling a major turning point in the Hundred Years War.

He says it doesn't matter. He buys us all a hotdog.

Rod shuffles cards with the confident ease of a man with a gambling problem. He cuts them and fans them out and flicks them from one hand to another like a seedy magician. Keeps giving me these shifty sideways looks. Sort of, wary. I probably shouldn't've shoved him quite so hard. I expect that's it. But I mean, it was self-defence. No one rips this cloak, it's vintage. Anyway, seems to have broken the ice a bit. We're here. Game of cards. Man to man.

'You like blackjack?'

'I like snap.'

We meet in the middle with rummy. Try to up the stakes a bit by betting on the winner. I've got my bus fare home and twenty-seven pee. Rod's got a six-pack of mini-rolls. You'd think we were playing for millions though. He is ruthless. And so gracious in victory.

'This is dismal. Pathetic. I've had stiffer competition from arthritis.'

'Don't rush me.'

'Come on.'

'Stop pressuring me. If you pressure me I make mistakes.'

'Have you even got seven cards there?'

'Course I have. God. Oh, hang on...'

Three – nil.

Eight – nil.

Eleven – nil. It's relentless.

He isn't for stopping though.

'Best of twenty-five,' he says. 'Your deal.'

I carry on. It isn't that bad. Not like there's something better going on downstairs. There's no comings or goings. This is pretty much as good as it gets round here till *Deal or No Deal*. There isn't much conversation. I would ask about his family, but he hasn't mentioned them and there's no photos or anything. I would ask about the neat man at the window but Rod never leaves his room. I would ask for a mini-roll but he's currently fondling them. At twenty-seven – nil, Rod stops. He's got this faraway look. I wonder what he is thinking. For a moment he seems sort of wistful.

'I'll have a shit now,' he says.

Back to wishing I'd never come.

'So are you like, a goth then?'

'Yes.'

Emma Collinson doesn't appear to have a rich inner-life. She carries on straightening her hair. Squirts some Frizz-Ease in my general direction. I move to the side a bit, look at her room. Every surface shimmers or sparkles or glistens or something. Like a shrine to the little gods of glitter. Sit there feeling drab.

'How come?'

'What d'you mean?'

'How come you're a goth?'

'I dunno. I just have these really dark thoughts. Like how everything is meaningless and that. And sort of: what's the point? Why don't we all just, you know.'

'Don't say that,' she laughs. A bit nervous. 'I've got enough worries tonight without that.'

I give her a sympathetic look.

'Is it your hair?'

That does it.

'No, Nick, it is not my hair.'

'Oh. Right.'

'For your information, my hair is frigging, perfect. It has taken me two hours to get it looking like this which is exactly how I want it to look.'

She clutches her straighteners, gives the mirror a tragic glance.

Like a sort of tearful Bonnie Tyler.
'It's very big,' I say.
I think she might kill me, but Greg arrives. He doesn't even
notice she's in a mood. Just stands in the doorway staring like
he's been let into Narnia. He's giving off this haze of lust and
Lynx Africa. Jingles his car keys for a bit, and then we go.
Nobody offers me the front seat, so I sit in the back and talk
about road accidents where the people in the passenger side get
crushed, disfigured or maimed.
She is too stupid to notice. Just keeps on looking at Greg.

'Give us a frigging hand.'
Rod's struggling to stand up. The hard thing is helping him
without appearing to help him.
'Would you stop pratting about?'
I heave him out of the chair. He's a big man and he's sort of
wedged. He knocks the deck of cards onto the floor and they
scatter. I stoop to gather them up.
'Leave them.'
We shuffle across to the commode. He barely lifts his feet up at
all. The soles of his slippers scuff the carpet and push the cards
along like a snowplough.
'You can sod off outside then now.'
There's something in his voice. I can't tell if it is caused by the
unspoken expression of gratitude or phlegm.
'I'll shout you when I'm done.'
It is quite a grim prospect for both of us.
I shut the door and bung in my iPod.
No one's about. I don't know why but, I sort of let my guard
down a bit.

Music: 'Push the Button' by Sugababes. NICK *shuffles about to*
it awkwardly, then stops.

We arrive at Smithy's house. The barbecue is dying down. It is
the Saturday after our exams and Neil and Davis are using the
last of the embers to burn six years' study of the German lan-
guage. The act of destruction brings an odd radiance to their
normally dull faces. It puts me in mind of *Lord of the Flies*. But
with umlauts.

Everyone else is pissed.

'Bring a bottle,' Smithy said. But the only thing I can find in our house is frigging mead. I notice nobody else is drinking a honey-based amber wine handmade by the monks of Lindisfarne, but at the same time, nobody says anything. I'm just marching to my own beat. It is like that when you wear eyeliner.

This song comes on. Greg sings the beginning and everyone laughs. He starts to dance like a twat. A couple of the other lads join in. I don't join in.

'Come on, Nick,' he says. 'You big gay. Be my Mutya.'

But Mutya's not even a Sugababe any more.

I sip my mead and yearn for oblivion. It doesn't take long. A group of girls appear in the garden drinking Bacardi Breezers suggestively. Emma Collinson starts bragging to everyone how her tits are now so big she qualifies for a breast reduction on the NHS. Greg dances over and looks down her top. I think, he's for it now. He is definitely getting a slap for that. But Emma just laughs.

'Cheeky,' she says. Stands up, starts dancing with him in what she clearly believes is a very erotic manner.

I can't watch.

They're not so much pushing the button as humping it.

Anyway.

Greg lost his virginity that night.

I didn't. I came home early and painted my bedroom black.

'I've just found your future husband.'

Greg bounds into my room. Looks a bit shocked at the paint-work. Flops onto my bed.

I stop reading *The Idiot*. Look at him instead.

'Really?'

'Yeah.'

'Go on then. What's he like?'

Greg grins:

'GAY!'

'Brilliant, sorted, I'll get my coat.'

'Alright, sarky. Thought that was the important bit.'

'Whatever. What you actually mean is you've found another random homosexual.'

'He's just nice, I suppose. That's more what I meant.'
'Nice?'
'Yeah. Nice.'
'Let me guess: skinny?'
'Yeah.'
'Intelligent?'
'Think so.'
'Bit plain?'
'S'pose... What?'
'Greg, if I wanted to shag someone like that, I'd have a wank.'
'Oh, for fuck's sake, Nick. You'd think if someone was nice and
smart and funny and sort of, gay, he'd be, you know. He'd be,
well, I dunno. Better than – '
'Better than nothing?'
'No.'
'What then?'
'Never mind. Doesn't matter.'
'No, tell me. Better than what? Better than what, Greg? Come
on. Tell me. Better than what?'
'Better than me.'
Greg stops.
'Better than you? Better than you?'
Greg coughs. Picks at a bit of skin down the side of his
fingernail.
'I should probably go.'
And he does. Downstairs. Out the door.
That's the last I heard from him really. Till sort of, this morning.
The postcard and that.
Finished *The Idiot* though. Bit of a let-down. Four out of ten,
probably.

Carol arrives at the top of the stairs, bent double and panting.
She mentions pushing the button. It crosses my mind that I am
in the presence of a low-level psychic.
Then I think: shit.
When we open the door, Rod is on the floor on his side in a sea
of playing cards. His trousers and pants are round his ankles. I
think he is unconscious. His face is grey and mottled and one
side of his mouth is covered in spit again. The seven of

diamonds is stuck to it. Carol takes his pulse, except he doesn't really seem to have one. He isn't breathing properly either. She rings downstairs, tells them to get an ambulance and send one of the nurses up. Asks me to help put Rod in the recovery position. I wonder if maybe this isn't a bit optimistic, but I do as she tells me. We move his arms and his legs, roll him onto a more comfy bit of his side. Make sure his airways are clear. Carol also pulls his pants up. I think this is something she's added to the first-aid procedure, but it is a nice touch all the same. She covers Rod with a blanket to keep him warm.
I am sweating like a bastard. And shaking like a bastard.
A male nurse comes in. Rod still has a tiny pulse so the nurse starts doing the breathing thing. Mouth-to-mouth. He has lovely arms, the nurse.
It is fascinating.
I can't believe it is only my third week and I'm actually getting to see somebody die.
Brilliant.
The nurse carries on with Rod's chest.
He says, It's touch-and-go. Me and Carol watch.

Something isn't right.
I am meant to be a creature of the shadows.
I listen to Marilyn Manson, and frequently wear a cloak.
Standing here, I'm looking right into the abyss. I couldn't have asked for a more existential situation. I should be loving it.
Everybody else is. There's at least three care assistants who weren't here before, desperate to help or just watch the nurse's arms. One of them has come from downstairs and is still wearing her party hat. I'm amazed she didn't bring cake. By the time the paramedics arrive it feels nearly festive.
But this isn't what I thought death would be like. This is...
I'm not enjoying this. Can't get into it at all.
I've decided, on balance, I would definitely prefer it if Rod didn't die.
I tell myself if Rod pulls round I'll make more of an effort. I'll take him downstairs, out into the garden. Have some sort of rummy marathon. I'll get him a box set of *Murder, She Wrote*. I dunno. I'll paint my bedroom magnolia.

'Come on, Rod,' I want to shout. 'Do it. Do it for Angela Lansbury.'
And then, just like that…

Pause.

You know.

It is 8.36 p.m. on the 15th of April 2008 and I am more distressed than I have ever been in my life. It's raining. I hammer on the door of Greg's shed till he opens it.
'Nick, what's up?'
(*Sobbing, gagging, hyperventilating.*) 'I've just come out to my mum and dad.'
'Oh God, are you alright?'
'No.'
'Shit. Were they mad?'
'No.'
'Did they chuck you out?'
'No, they were really supportive.'
'What?'
'They said they already knew, just want me to be happy and that.'
'Nick, it's alright, calm down.'
'I can't.'
'Come in here.'
'I keep being sick.'
'Oh. Maybe outside then.'
'No, I'm fine now.'
'You don't sound fine.'
'I don't know why I'm being such a knob.'
Greg helps me inside the shed. Half of it is his mum's potting shed and half of it is where he does weights so it smells pretty odd in there. Compost and testosterone. I think of it as composterone, which doesn't help. His T-shirt is soaking with sweat, but I am crying in that snotty way you can't fake so, not really in a position to complain. He sits me down on his bench thing and gives me without doubt the worst hug of my life. It is so tight I can't breathe and when I do manage a gulp of air it reeks of composterone. I nearly gag.

But it helps.

I think about that while I'm walking downstairs.

How you expect the whole world to change. That is only right, because something enormous has happened to you. You have changed. But it doesn't. People saw it coming; they were ready for it; they are not really bothered anyway. Everything goes on the same as it always did. And that takes some getting used to.

NICK*'s eyeliner is a bit smudged. He has acquired a pink balloon.*

They are having a whale of a time in the activities room. Music and joy and so on. It makes me think of *Titanic*, before the iceberg. And I suppose I am the iceberg. I enter the room like the bearer of bad news. This isn't unusual for me, it's sort of a way of life, but today I am actually bearing bad news and I have to say I don't enjoy it like I thought. Don't drag it out at all. I'm not even tempted to put up my hood like a sinister monk. I just tell them:

'Rod is dead.'

Silence.

I feel a little bit like Friedrich Nietzsche.

Only sadder. And more, hollow. My bottom lip wobbles. I don't know where to look.

They take the news well. The general opinion seems to be: about time. 'He was a bit of a tyrant at Scrabble,' they say. That doesn't surprise me.

But I am still feeling a bit out of sorts. I make my excuses. Elsie insists I take a balloon home. As a child of Satan I am loathe to accept such a frivolous item but I'm worried I never see her again. All life seems to hang by such delicate threads this afternoon. I take it. It is pink.

Feel like a right tit at the bus stop.

Look back up at the home. The neat man's still at the window. His outline. Hasn't moved. Hat and coat and suitcase. Looks at his watch. Goes back to waiting. I'm glad to see the number 23.

And then it happens. Sitting on the bus, sticky in the heat, with my cloak on and a frigging pink balloon held a bit too tight in my left hand, messy eyeliner and the thought of Rod sat by himself in that room, determined not to enjoy anything, not even my bloody muffin, or even just on the floor dying with nobody giving a toss, I realise something.

The kitchen is empty, but everyone is home.
Lizzie's doing Geri Halliwell's yoga DVD in the front room.
Like a –
I wonder if she would appreciate a balloon.
My mum and dad are celebrating their victory over the French by having noisy sex upstairs. They giggle and the armour clanks.
I put in my iPod and try to be pleased for them. Remind myself it's only once a year.
This is the best I can do.
Small steps.
I am feeling so much, I dunno, stuff for everyone. Stuff you can't say.
I will do my best to communicate it by not being a twat.
Hang up my cloak one last time. Look for magnolia paint.

NOTES FOR FIRST TIME ASTRONAUTS

Notes for First Time Astronauts was first performed by
Tom Wells at Soho Theatre, London, on 5 October 2009, as part
of Paines Plough's LATER programme, directed by Ben Webb.

You mustn't wank in space. It goes everywhere.

They tell you that before you set off, just in case. A humourless doctor sits you down. And you sort of think: I've managed everything NASA's thrown at me so far, I really hope that won't be my downfall. Just cross my fingers or something. Pretend I'm Buddhist.

After four days on the International Space Station things look a bit different.

Everywhere you turn there's these brilliant, chiselled, scientific hunks just floating around like the seeds off a dandelion clock. With Russian accents. And, shoulders. Making witty observations about the cosmos. And then me trying to focus on my soldering. It is getting increasingly hard though. In my pants. And it's not the sort of environment where something like that goes unnoticed. Conditions are cramped enough. So I decide to take action. Put my circuit board down and as it drifts listlessly away along the corridor I head back to my capsule for a bit. Just to sort of, sort myself out.

It happens unexpectedly.

Lying there, hermetically sealed in my Smarties tube of a bedroom, hurtling through space at 17,227 miles per hour, I think about you. It's been years but. I start wondering what you'll be up to. Sitting in a bedsit in Huddersfield looking at drizzle. Pairing your socks. Watching a Tesco Value biriyani in its solitary orbit of the microwave. That sort of thing.

They were right of course. It does go everywhere.

*

For weeks after you've been to the beach, sand turns up in unexpected places. And when you worked in that pub kitchen you said the same thing happened with cress. But this takes the piss. It's been a good two hours and I'm still swatting little flecks of it away like midges at a picnic. Or karma, possibly. If anything it is more distracting than the hunks. The soldering's nearly done though. Which means one thing:

Tomorrow we will be walking on the Moon.

I mean, I'm only there to hold the camera, but still. Pretty good going for someone from Huddersfield. Someone who can't even parallel park.

Breathtaking really.

Thinking about that, the circuit board's finished in no time.

*

I can see our old school from space. Our old science lab even. I'm not a hundred per cent but I think our project about levers is still up on the back wall. Yellowing with age. Mr Benson seems as incompetent as ever. NASA have managed to organise a live satellite link-up the day before a moonwalk, he's struggling to cope with a webcam. There's the usual clunking and clattering and black pixellated bits, and then, at last, I can see them. Thirty unimpressed Year Tens, and Mr Benson grinning.

He can't believe it. One of his. In space.

Everyone else looks a bit underwhelmed. It was meant to be inspirational. Show them what you can achieve if you knuckle down in your GCSEs. But they're not really bothered. They just want to bung in their iPods and grope each other. It's not everyone's dream, I know that. As one of the lads on the back row loudly points out: 'NASA is gay.' That gets a laugh. He tries again: 'Mate, do you bum each other in space?' Mr Benson is looking a bit strained. 'That's enough, Gavin.'

One of the Russians appears through the hatch to see what all the noise is. He's excited, asks if he can stay to practise his English. I give him a warning look but he gets offended.

Tells me: 'I speak almost perfect English.'

Unfortunately, the Year Tens of Huddersfield do not.

The Russian looks confused. 'What do they mean: bumming?'

Gavin demonstrates with a helpful mime.

Then, out of nowhere, we notice a change in their faces. The noise stops. I wonder if something is wrong with the satellite link-up. If it's frozen, or the connection's gone. But it all seems fine. They're just silent all of a sudden. Captivated.

And from the back Gavin pipes up: 'What the fuck is that?'

*

I fell in love in that classroom. Not just with astrophysics.

Remember it?

We're seventeen. I've stayed behind to do extra work. You're there for detention. We're coiling wire around graphite rods and Benson's left us to it. You're big and clumsy and stupid. I can't help feeling Physics A level is a bit of a waste when you've got 'shelf-stacker' written all over you. Spelt wrong. You come over and stand next to me. I don't need this. I'm in training for the British science Olympiad.

'Everyone's saying you're gay.'

I blush bright red which is not quite the denial I was hoping for. But, you're smiling.

'I wondered if, sort of. Maybe we could, you know. I mean, if you...'

I don't know what to say.

'Are you kidding?'

You're not kidding.

'But, I mean. I should probably get on with...'

I gesture towards my electromagnets.

You take the solenoid out of my hand. Put it down on the bench carefully.

I'm smiling a bit now. Can't help it.

But, anyway. Hold that thought.

*

Hovering in front of the webcam, about the size of a large pea, bobbing about, ever so slightly changing shape, is what can only be described as a glob of my jizz.

It must look massive to the schoolkids. Perspective and that. Like a spermy planet.

This never happened to Buzz Aldrin.

They keep asking: 'What is it? What is it?'

Even Mr Benson's asking.

And the Russian's pretty curious too. According to NASA's guidelines, a rogue liquid is a cause for alarm. Bit of an understatement in this case.

I don't know what to say. I've always been shit at lying. Rack my brains, frantically, trying to come up with some vaguely plausible explanation. It's no good though. The best I can do is:

'Yoghurt?'

The Russian sees straight through this. Dairy products are forbidden on the International Space Station. I'm pretty sure most of the lads back in Huddersfield have their doubts an' all. I can see them thinking: 'Yoghurt. Right. That old chestnut.'

And then another thought gets into their little heads. I see that spark of inspiration happening. Gavin is first in. Starts the chant.

'Eat it. Eat it. Eat it.'

'Oh no, I couldn't really.'

'Go on, mate, eat it. Eat it. Eat it.'

'No, honestly, I don't know how long it's been...'

'Eat it eat it eat it.'

The kids are getting out of control. Shouting, laughing, feet stamping. So loud. Mr Benson looks at me. Begging. It wouldn't hurt, he seems to say. Please.

There's nothing to be done.

I look at it.

Steel myself.

Lean forward.

Shut my eyes and close my mouth around it.

And, perhaps it is just in my head but. It tastes a little bit like Tesco Value biriyani.

*

In space, I have trouble sleeping. You have to sort of strap yourself into bed. I should be excited about tomorrow but, I know how quickly news gets round. That Russian couldn't wait to spread it. By morning I'll be sacked or something. Off the mission. Even if I'm not, I can hardly go a-moonwalking when the entire scientific community knows I've just gobbled my own jizz in front of thirty underprivileged Northern schoolkids.

Drift off eventually though. Sort of.

You meet me at the edges of sleep. We're seventeen still. But this time you've got me. Held. Safe and that. I'm shaking a bit. You tell me: 'We don't have to.'

'No, I want to.'

'Sure?'

You start as gently as you can.

But I mean, even that. It fucking wrecks and. I am so tense, I'm not relaxed at all. Without meaning to, I sort of gasp a bit. I'm really not sure I can, you know...

You stop.

'You alright?'

'Not really.'

And you just know then. Carefully pull it out.

As first times go, it's not spectacular. Not even sure it counts but. Still.

Something to think about while you fall asleep.

*

I suppose it is beautiful, but. I'm really only here to hold the camera.

The rest of the crew are doing these massive leaps and somersaults and laughing. Still going on about, you know.

Sort of takes the shine off a bit.

It is pretty lonely on the Moon to be honest. Big and quiet and slow and white and cold. Dusty.

You are 238,855 miles away. In Huddersfield.

I was that fucking determined to get away from Huddersfield. Better things and that.

Look out across the whole of space.

Not much there.

Mostly it's just. Space.

Wonder if all this was worth it.

Sort of think: probably not, really.

I miss you.

Hope you're doing alright.

A Nick Hern Book

Me, As A Penguin first published in Great Britain as a paperback original in 2010 by Nick Hern Books Limited, 14 Larden Road, London W3 7ST in association with Milan Govedarica

Cover image by Jan Will
Cover designed by Ned Hoste, 2H

Typeset by Nick Hern Books, London
Printed in the UK by CLE Print Ltd, St Ives, Cambs, PE27 3LE

A CIP catalogue record for this book is available from the British Library

ISBN   978 1 84842 104 2